*"Hell and The Stovepipe"*
*"World War II Monkey"*
*"Black Culture Influence"*

# *The*
# *Story*
# *Of*
# *My*
# *Life*

Homer Williams

iUniverse, Inc.
New York   Bloomington

**The Story of My Life**
**Hell and the Stovepipe, World War II**
**Monkey, Black Culture Influence**

*iUniverse books may be ordered through booksellers or by contacting:*

*iUniverse*
*1663 Liberty Drive*
*Bloomington, IN 47403*
*www.iuniverse.com*
*1-800-Authors (1-800-288-4677)*

*Because of the dynamic nature of the Internet, any Web addresses or
links contained in this book may have changed since publication and may
no longer be valid.*

*ISBN: 978-1-4401-2830-1 (pbk)*
*ISBN: 978-1-4401-2831-8 (ebk)*

*Printed in the United States of America*

*iUniverse rev. date: 4/7/2009*

# DEDICATION

This book is dedicated to the most important people in my life. My wife, Gloria, has been a faithful helpmate for fifty two years. Her enthusiasm for living and vibrant smile cheers any room she enters. My three sons, Timothy, Jonathan, and Christopher have been the ultimate in the expectation of any father. The pride they have brought me is difficult to properly record on paper. Their wives, Mary, Cindy, and Tammy complete their lives and have given Gloria and me eight wonderful grandchildren.

*We all come from the past, and children*
*ought to know what it was that went into*
*their making, to know that life is a*
*braided cord of humanity stretching up*
*from time long gone, and that it cannot*
*be defined by the span of a single journey*
*from diaper to shroud.*

*Russell Baker, Growing Up*

# Contents

# INTRODUCTION

I decided to write my life story so my children, grandchildren and other relatives would have a feeling for the heritage that I felt that I had received. I considered it necessary to record many of the events that made up a great portion of my life.

I utilized some oral and written stories from my parents, sisters and brothers. I also utilized Ancestry.com on the internet to research incidents of the Civil War. I had two great-grandfathers to serve in this war. My mother gave me some very old documents in an old shoe box that I was able to utilize and I attempted to record many episodes of my life as I had recalled them while growing up. I also utilized a very old newspaper that I have.

I have experienced many stories that have been handed down through the years. Many go back prior to the Civil War. I do know that many stories from my older brothers and sisters have been forgotten and no longer exist.

There seems to be a lack of kinship today on the part of so many families in our society. It is important for me to write my autobiography so my children, grandchildren and as many relatives as possible have an understanding of kinship with our heritage. I know my brothers and sisters and their children will get a feel for the heritage handed down from those who have gone before us.

In writing about yesterday and today, I am attempting to put down an account of my life that will provide history for tomorrow.

We know that there is a genetic connection among families, however something that is possessed as a result of ones natural situation or birth - our heritage, gives us a quality of being kin.

I hope you enjoy reading this story of my life.

*Homer M. Williams*
*Fort Mill-Indian Land, SC*
*May 2008*
*Formerly, Oak Hill, Ohio*

# Chapter 1

## "It Wasn't Santa Screaming"

As you leave Morhead, Kentucky, going east on Route 32, you come to a road that is called North Fork Tripplet. Eighteen miles up this hollow lived my father and mother, George and Beulah Williams with eight other children. They lived on a  farm that had been given to him by his father.  In an upper bedroom of this log house, Christmas morning - December 25, 1932, a  screaming boy was delivered by midwife Maude Riley. When I got older, my oldest sister, Ida Mae, said that their expectations were that Santa would quietly slip into the house and leave candy and fruit for all of them, but to their surprise they were awakened by the screaming of a new baby brother that spoiled their nights sleep.

The Dow Jones for December 24, 1932 was 57 and the president elect was Franklin Delano Roosevelt. Railroads seemed to be improving and a definite uptrend in work was occurring. My father had obtained a job with The Chesapeake and Ohio Railroad Company.

The automobile industry was really picking up with 200,000 families whose men had returned to work on intensive production of the 1933 models. This was stated in the San Francisco Chronicle, December 24, 1932, (data from Detroit). There was another 50,000 to be added to the payrolls by mid-June 1933.

The Senate of the United States was expected to approve a 3.2 percent beer bill after the Christmas break. The beer would travel in glass bottles as large as box cars. The cars were prepared to carry two 3000 gallon insulated tanks, constructed of steel and lined with glass from brewers to buyers all over the country.

On December 24, 1932, Mildred "Babe" Diedrickson was ranked as the worlds greatest woman athlete by the experts. Another interesting sports event was in basketball. Coach Cam Henderson of Davis & Elkins College in West Virginia, was the winner of the Intercollegiate Atlantic Seaboard. He was to play United Athletic Club in San Francisco December 26. 1932. Davis and Elkins College had been playing barnstorming games across the country. I give this interesting tidbit as you will learn later on about when I met Coach Cam.

In movies, Edward G Cantor, had "The Kid from Spain, Edward G Robinson, "Silver Bells", and Richard Dix, "The Conquerors". Samuel Goldwyn said the picture industry needs fifty good pictures a year and no more. He felt there were only a limited number of actors and actresses that were really capable of making winning pictures.

One of the new books that was coming out was by Winston Churchill, "Amid These Storms". Some of the

Comics in newspapers were, The Gumps, Moon Mullins, Gasoline Alley. Jo Palooka, Hawkshaw The Detective, and Captain and The Kids.

In the spring of 1933 my father and mother left me with my older sister, Ida Mae and they took a trip to The Chicago Exposition in Chicago. They took Kenneth, my 20 month older brother with them. Ida told me in later years that she was responsible for weaning me as I had been breast fed the past five months. She said it was really a great task and she would get irritated with me and sometimes pinch me to see if I could scream any louder! This must have been an interesting time for my parents in that they found time to travel to Chicago, even with the responsibilities of the new baby in the family. They were traveling on a pass that dad received as a benefit for working on the railroad. I still think about them leaving that hollow to pursue cultural events in the big city.

# Chapter 2

## PARENTS, GRANDPARENTS AND GREAT GRANDPARENTS

My father is George Washington Williams from Rowan County, Kentucky. He was born in 1888 and they lived on a farm on North Fork Tripplet. Beulah Estella Fite was from Lewis County, Kentucky and was born in 1893. She came to Rowan County to stay with an aunt for the summer. There were revival meetings being held at the Hardyman church grounds and my father said he saw her there and told his mother that she would be his wife someday. They were married in 1909, he at the age of twenty-one and mother was sixteen.

Dad was a very hard worker. I recall one cold winter, the snow was very deep on the ground and he said that he was going to make some extra money for Christmas. He had a man to help him cut logs from up in the hills on the farm. He had a team of oxen pull the large logs from the hills to the wood yard near our house. Dad used an axe to flatten the logs on two sides for cross ties. He and this man loaded the wagon with cross ties to be sold to the railroad in Morhead, Kentucky. He said they paid him 50 cents per crosstie. I think they could take sixteen cross ties per load and he had five loads. This trip was eighteen miles, one way.

Dad's father was Thomas Jefferson Williams from Johnson County, Kentucky. He was born in 1838, in Virginia and married Easter Ellen Lawson from Scott County Virginia. She was born March 2, 1850. Grandfather Williams passed away in 1909 and Grandmother Williams passed away in 1922. They are buried in "The Williams Cemetery", North Fork Triplet, Kentucky. Grandfather Williams left one acre of land for a cemetery on the farm he gave Dad. We still visit there today, even though we moved away in 1942. Grandmother Williams' father, William B. Lawson was from Scott County, Virginia. He was a private in the Civil War for the South and "slipped" away. He left for Kentucky because he thought they were neutral and no one would have to fight. Later on the Governor of Kentucky said regiments would be formed to fight in the war. There were regiments forming for the North and Regiments forming for the South. How interesting all of this is. Mother left an old shoe box with 1850 tax records from Virginia and Kentucky. There was a Parole of Honor in the box. This Parole of Honor is signed by Great Grandfather Lawson, (his x), 31$^{st}$ day of March 1864, A.C. Tober, Justice of the Peace, Carter County, Kentucky. I have this original copy. I did research of William B. Lawson from Ancestry.com, Full Context of American Civil War Soldiers. His service record said he enlisted as a Private on 6 September 1862 in Scott, VA, in <u>Company A, 25 Cavalry Regiment Virginia</u>. He reported sick on the 15th of December 1862 at Emory And Henry Hospital. He deserted on 9 December 1863. The source for this is The Virginia Regimental Histories Series. (VARosterC) Published in 1987. Benjamin Franklin Fite, my mother's grandfather was from Brown, County, Ohio. He fought for the North in the Civil War. On November 25, 1863, Union soldiers assaulted and carried the seemingly impregnable Confederate position on Missionary Ridge. One of the Confederacy's two major armies was routed. It was on this day that great grandfather Fite got killed. He was 35 years old and with Company G, 59th Ohio Volunteer Infantry. He left a wife, Bathsheba and three children. My mother's father was one of the children, John Benjamin Fite.

Grandfather John Benjamin Fite Sr., married Sarah Ellen Havens from Morgan County, Kentucky. They had twelve children, my mother being the ninth child. They lived in Lewis County, Kentucky.

My grandmother, Sarah Ellen Havens Fite was born March 25, 1857 at Mt. Sterling, Morgan County, Ky. A story that my oldest sister wrote down and left a copy for me, was about grandmother Sarah, when she was a young girl went to the Kansas Territory with all of her sisters, brothers and parents to homestead. All of them came back except one of her sisters, Rebecca. She stayed and reared a family in Coffeyville. She set up a bicycle repair shop to make extra money. Rebecca told a story that she remembers seeing the James Boys riding into town. After my grandmother Sarah married grandfather John Fite, she wanted to go out West again. Grandfather Fite said he would go and see if he liked it or not. While he was there a large storm came up and the homesteaders were looking for a small boy that got lost. They found him and they said it was a miracle that he was alive. His name was Finnesay Favorite.

When grandfather Fite returned home, the baby they were expecting was born, February 15, 1880, a boy. And he thinking it a good omen, named him Finnesay Favorite Fite. He told grandmother Fite that he would not live in Kansas if he was given the whole Territory. You will see mother's brother, Finnesay Favorite Fite, in the chapter of Uncles and Aunts.

An old "hand me down story" that was told to some of the older children was that Grand Paw Fite grew tired of farming and got the roaming bug in his bones. He left his family and headed West, where he stayed with the Mormons for some time. When he came back to his family, he left the farming to them and he took care of the saw mill. He was an avid reader, a great fiddler, dancer and excellent singer. The family had farm animals, vegetable garden, fruit orchards, ground their own meal, spun wool and made all the clothes for the children.

# Chapter 3

## MY BROTHERS AND SISTERS
## HOW LUCKY I AM

My oldest brother, George Thomas Williams, was born on September 11, 1910 at Triplet, Kentucky. This was on mothers seventeenth birthday. He went to Hardyman Grade School near where we lived. When he finished the eighth grade, mother and dad sent him to Breckenridge Training School at Morhead College. He passed the test and the next term of school, 1929-30, he was the teacher of the Hardyman school. He was nineteen years old. I have the little booklet he gave out to the children of the school. His picture is on the front of it.

He served in the Merchant Marines during World War II. After he got out of service, he married Roslyn Feinberg, from Hammond, Indiana. They lived in Cincinnati, Ohio for a couple of years. He decided to leave for awhile and Roslyn came to our house in West Virginia and lived with us for about a year. She had their baby, Karen Sue with her. Mother took care of the baby while Roslyn worked at the Maiden Form Plant in Huntington, WV. The bus left about 5:00 AM and returned in the evening about 5:00 PM. Roslyn would say to mother, I know George loves me and he will call me. About a year went by and George called and asked Roslyn to come to Seattle, Washington. He was working at Boeing airplane factory. Roz left to be with George. They had another girl, Melinda Sue after they moved to Bellflower, California and he worked at Boeing there. He passed away in1982 and is buried in Whittier, CA. Three sisters and I went there for the funeral. An old, old song that I heard many times when at revival in the one room school house in KY, was "The Church in the Wildwood", my brother George had requested this as one of the songs that they played at the funeral. I always looked up to my oldest brother as such a role model and an outstanding individual. He was mother's first son and I was her last son.

My oldest sister, Ida Mae was born in 1912. She is the sister that kept me when mom, dad & my twenty month old brother went to the World's Exposition (Fair) in the summer of 1933. Ida married a man from the area where we lived in 1934. He got killed in an accident with a timber truck during their first year of marriage. At the end of WWII, Ida married Scott Sage from Willard, Ohio. They lived in Cincinnati, Ohio and later in Point Pleasant and Pleasant View, WV. They had two daughters, Sheryl and Gloria. Ida is buried in the Enon Cemetery at Salt Rock, WV.

Loren Williams was born February 9, 1914 in Lewis County, KY. He worked for the C&O Railway and was in Huntington WV where he met Virginia McCallister and married her.

They had three children, Arlene, Jean and David. They lived in Hurricane, WV and he worked for the Carbide and Carbon Chemical Plant in Southe Charleston, WV.

Loren taught me how to drive. He had a 1939 Chevrolet four door and I thought it was such a great deal to drive that car. I had to take my drivers test in Hamlin, WV. This was the county seat of Lincoln County. Edgar Jennings (EJ) Midkiff took me over to get my test in his grandfather's car, a 1949 Chevrolet. I still have my first driver's license that was issued to me in 1950. Loren passed away in 1985 and is buried in Enon Cemetery at Salt Rock, WV.

Cartmal Williams was born in 1918. He enlisted in the Army 19 September 1940. He was in the 82nd Airborne and then the 101st Airborne Division. He was in Bastogne when the German General asked the US to surrender and Gen. McCaullif's answer was "Nuts". After Cartmal got out of the Army, he married Hattie Hensley from Louisa, KY. They had six children, Sandy, Judy, Bonnie, Carolyn, George and Kirby. Cartmal retired from the C&O Railway. He passed away in 1992 and is buried in Louisa, KY.

Lorena Williams was born in 1922. She finished Hardyman grade school. In 1940-41 she went to Berea College at Berea, KY. During WWII, she worked in Cincinnati, OH in a defense plant with my older sister, Ida Mae. After the war, she married Elmer D. Barbour. They had three children, Paula, April and Charles. Elmer passed away in 1972 and Lorena in 2005.

Harold Williams was born in 1924 and died as an infant. He is buried in the Williams Cemetery.

Mildred Williams was born in 1927. She married Lon Lewis from West Hmlin, WV. This was in 1947. We had moved from Kentucky in 1942. Mildred had worked at Sylvania Plant in Huntington, WV. They had three children, Tamara, Lon III, and Menina. Lon II was in the Army during WWII. He is buried in the Enon Cemetery at Salt Rock, WV.

Kenneth Williams was born February 8, 1931. He was one year ahead of me in school. He graduated from Guyan Valley HS at Pleasant View, WV in 1950. He joined the Marines a few months after graduation and fought in Korea and was awarded the Purple Heart. He came home after he returned from Korea and married his high school sweetheart, Jo Ann McComas from Hubbell, WV. They had two children, Pamela and Kenneth. He retired from the Southern Railway and lives in Ft. Lauderdale, FL.

Joyce Williams was born in 1935 in Kentucky. She graduated from Guyan Valley HS in 1954. She married Paul Porter from Huntington, WV, in 1955. They had two children, Mark and Paula. They live in Tampa, Florida..

# Chapter 4

## AUNTS AND UNCLES

I was the tenth child in a family of eleven, and my father was the youngest of eleven children, and mother was from a family of twelve, her being the ninth child. This resulted in few opportunities for me to get to know my aunts and uncles. Now more about dad's brothers & sisters

Dad's brothers and sisters: Uncle John Williams was born in 1866 in Rowan County, KY. He married Hariett, and moved to Maben, WV. Aunt Martha was born April 3, 1869 in Rowan County. She married Barnie Kinder. She passed away in 1944 and is buried in the Williams Cemetery. Aunt Mazilpha Williams was born in 1871. She married Randy Andy and they had five children. Her husban, Randy left her with the five children and ran away with her brother's wife and her child and ended up in Seattle, Washington. The child's name was Zenith. Randy returned many years later to Cincinnati, where Mazilphia was living with one of her children. He begged Mazilphia to take him back and she repeated a saying that she had related for many years, "Randy, I would not allow you to piss on the ground of my farm if it saved your life, so you can leave". She passed away in 1944 in Cincinnati, OH. Uncle Marion Williams was born in 1870. I have no other information about him. Uncle Reuben Williams was born in Rowan County in 1874. He passed away in Willmore, WV in 1939.

Uncle Thomas Williams was born in 1875 in Rowan County, KY. Aunt Bell Williams England was born in 1877 in Rowan Co. KY. Aunt Margaret was born in 1878. Uncle Henry Williams was born in 1881 and passed away on North Fork Tippet, KY, 1956. My wife, Gloria and I took dad to the funeral in Kentucky. Uncle Henry is buried in the Williams Cemetery.

Mother's brothers and sisters: Aunt Jennie Williams Fite was born in 1885. She married Finnasy Fite, a brother of my mother. Aunt Jennie passed away in Lewis County, KY in 1945.

Uncle J.B. Fite was born January 5, 1876 in Carter County, KY. Uncle Charles Franklin Fite was born Dec 31, 1877. Uncle Finnesy Favorite Fite, born February 15, 1880. Aunt Hattie Fite was born January 31, 1882. Uncle George Fite, born March 12, 1884. Uncle Thomas B Fite born July 22, 1886. Uncle Lewis E Fite, born October 31, 1888. Uncle Joel M. Fite, born July 19, 1891. (My mother Beulah Fite was born September 11, 1893). Uncle Jennings B. Fite, was born September 4, 1895, Aunt Jeannette B. Fite born October 26, 1897 and Uncle Julus J Fite, was born November 19, 1900..

I remember Aunt Jeannette coming to our house in Kentucky before Christmas in 1938. She had a suitcase and two shopping bags. The shopping bags were on the floor in the dining room and she was looking at a few items she had for the children and was bending down looking in the bags and singing, "I found a hiding place, a blessed hiding place", I forget the rest of the words but I remember that she gave us gifts! How happy we were.

Uncle Julus came to our house in West Virginia in 1945. He had a 1939 Chevrolet and he stayed for a couple of days and left. I met him only two times.

# Chapter 5

## EARLY MEMORIES OF TOYS

One of my first memories of receiving a toy was a red Rambler wagon. The picture of this wagon is included in the picture section. My older brother, Kenneth and a neighbor boy, Harold Nickels are with me. Harold and I are in the wagon. I was about three years old at the time.

In 1937 my oldest brother, George, who was working in Cincinnati, Ohio, came home for Christmas. I didn't know it at the time but he was the Santa Claus. He left candy, fruit, and a toy for each one of us. He went out the front door. Later my brother George came in the back door. We told him that Santa had visited our house. He said he had been out to the toilet and on his way back he found a jar of peanut butter and bet that Santa lost it out of his bag.

I will never forget that toy. It was a small monkey, standing on his hind legs, holding a small mirror with one hand, holding a comb over his head and combing his hair with the other hand. You would wind him up and he would start turning around, looking in the mirror and combing his hair.

We had just been in our newly built house for a short time. Just off one of the bedrooms upstairs, the area wasn't finished. There were a few boards laying on the 2 x 8's and mother said this was off limits. We sometime slipped to this "off limits" area. Once I went there and was playing and dropped my favorite toy down between the 2 x 4's, going all the way down to the first floor. I have always wondered if someone ever found my favorite toy when they were possibly repairing the house. There has been one family that has owned the farm and a son inherited it from his father and mother. No one lives in the house now and it is very much in disrepair.

# Chapter 6

## THE ONE ROOM SCHOOL

In 1939, I started in the first grade at the Hardyman Grade School, which was about one-half mile from our house. This was a one room school with a large stove in the middle of the room with a stove pipe going up through the ceiling. The stove burned wood to heat the building during cold weather. Some of the parents cut the wood and stacked it near the building for our use. There were windows on one side and one end of the room. If you set in a seat near the window on that side of the room, you could see the dirt road that was nearby. A very large oak tree was at the end of the schoolyard where we the younger children played.

The water that we had for drinking was obtained from Mr. Nickels, a neighbor nearby.

We had a large bucket that set on a lower shelf in the back of the room. There was a tin cup with a handle on it that we drank the water from.

Our outdoor toilets were about fifty yards away from the building. As I remember, they were located near some pine trees.

I vividly remember a couple of things that happened during my second year of school. Clinton Stacey, a friend of mine set next to me at a table at one end of the room. We earlier grades set at a table together. The older children set at the old school desks.

One day Clinton and I decided to imitate our older brothers who chewed tobacco. We would spit in a chair between us at this table. The teacher caught us and asked us why we were doing this. We told her that we were only imitating our older brothers who chewed tobacco. She told us to stay in during recess and the others were excused except one boy she asked to go get a switch. He came back, gave her the switch and went outside. She came toward us and we ran around the room and we began to cry. She had tears in her eyes and said she hated to do this and she hit us each once and a boy was looking in a window from the side of the room and she got more upset about that than what we did. She called all of them back into the building from recess.

At the end of the year, there was a special day for recitations. Parents would come to the building to see their children perform. We younger students would stand on a table to recite our work. My mother had worked with me on the recitation that she wanted me to say. I said, "I'm not very big and I'm not very tall but I have something to tell you all, I don't have much to say but I may grow up to be your president some day". What an applause!

During my third grade, the teacher for the school, Mrs Thompson, from Morhead, Ky, roomed and boarded at our house. One of the rules my mother had was if you got a spanking at school, you received one when you came home.

During the spring of the year, my friend, Clinton Stacey, got mad at me. We were playing under the large oak tree at the end of the school yard. He hit me on the back a number of times and my nose started bleeding. The teacher gave us a whipping. When I came home, my mother had already heard about it. An older student had gone to Mr Nickel's house for drinking water for the school and told Mrs. Nickels. Mrs Nickels went over to our house and told mother. My mother used a belt to discipline me with, that was her rule, get a whipping by the teacher and I give you one. My older brother, Cartmal got me on his lap and showed me a silver dollar and told me that it was mine if I went to school the next day and beat the ?+## out of Clinton. Mother heard this and told Cartmal he shouldn't do that because he will get a whipping at school by the teacher and one when he gets home. I thought that was a great prize, the silver dollar. The next day I whipped Clinton, got whipped by the teacher and when I came home, Cartmal asked me what happened, I told him and he gave me the silver dollar. He said mom, he doesn't get another whipping, the teacher spanked him and he didn't start the first fight. Mom didn't whip me & I thought I was rich!

We took our lunch to school every day. It usually consisted of a biscuit with melted butter on it and jelly, a biscuit with sausage or ham or bacon and egg on it. Each day the lunch also contained a piece of pie, cake or cookies. My friend Clinton and I usually walked out beyond the softball field and ate our lunch. We sat near the dirt road that passes by in the large sage brush growing near the road. One lunch hour he and I decided to cuss like we had heard our older brother cuss. We just called out many cuss words that we had heard. That afternoon when I got home, mother whipped me with the belt. I asked her why she was doing this, and she said Mrs. Walters said she was coming up the road near the school at lunchtime and Clinton and Homer gave her a good cussing out. She told mother she never heard such cuss words as they were using. After this episode calmed down, I asked mom if I could tell her why Mrs. Walters heard the cuss words? She said ok. I told her we were trying to imitate our older brothers. Mom said I didn't think you would cuss Mrs. Walters, however you are not to use cuss words, even if you are repeating your older brother Cartmal!

# Chapter 7

## MY SPECIAL CHAPTER, GROWING TO THE AGE OF NINE

As I thought about what I wanted to include in this chapter, I felt I would list some of my experiences growing up to the age of nine, on a large farm in th hills of Kentucky.

One of the experiences I had at an early age was my mother getting a newspaper from Cincinnati, Ohio. This arrived by our mail carrier who delivered the mail on a horse. An older brother that worked in Cincinnati had the paper sent to mother. Of all the stories she read to us in the newspaper, one stood out very vividly - the Hindenberg explosion, with pictures. This was in May 1937. The Cincinnati Post showed a picture of it exploding and falling toward the ground. I was very curious as to why people wished to travel in a balloon, which I didn't think was a safe way to travel.

Most of all the food we ate was raised on the farm. Mother cooked on a wood burning kitchen stove with a food warming closet above and at the back of the stove.

There was a water tank on the side that heated the water when we cooked. Mom had hot water to do the dishes without heating the water on top of the stove.

I was not knowledgeable of electricity. We had lamps that used kerosene, we called it coal oil. Mother always cleaned the lamp shades daily. This consisted of removing any dark carbon that may have formed inside of the shades. If this film was permitted to build up inside the lamp shade, it would reduce the amount of light that was given off in a room and it was more difficult to read if you didn't have the brighter light. We visited neighbors that had shades that were covered with this carbon soot and the rooms were very poorly lighted. Mom would tell us she couldn't understand why they didn't clean their lamp shades. Mom said it was so much easier to read in a room with bright light coming through clean shades. In later years, I realized that many of the neighbors never read much.

There were many disadvantages of not having refrigeration. One was that the butter would melt. We put the butter in a bucket and lowered it in the well and it stayed firm. We also had a spring that came into the cellar house, which was located a distance away. We would put milk in covered pails, in the cold water located in the corner of the cellar, and had cold milk to drink.

Every fall of the year, after cold weather arrived, our father slaughtered hogs. He usually had help from a neighbor or two, as dad was to return the favor when they slaughtered hogs. The fat that was removed from the hogs were rendered into lard by mother. She would put the fat portions of the meat into large pans and put into the oven and the drippings, fat, was removed from these portions. The lard in liquid form was permitted to cool slightly, then poured into five and ten pound pails. These pails were stored in the cellar house for use later on.

The pieces of fat in which the lard was removed from, were then called "cracklins". These were put into pails and sealed for later use. The "cracklins" were put into cornbread. This was a favorite of mine, cracklin cornbread, how delicious it was.

We assisted our mother in the grinding, (using a hand operated sausage grinder), of the meats from the hogs that she utilized into the making of the sausage. Mom always insisted that a shoulder of a hog go into the making of the sausage, that it made the sausage so much better. Dad didn't agree with this, as he wanted to save all of the shoulders for later use. You know who won this disagreement, mom!

Mother had a unique way of storing some of the sausage. She would take an old white clean sheet, cut out squares and sew them together to make a tube to store some of the sausage in. The sausage would fill up these tubes, which were about two pounds of sausage, and stored in the smoke house. Mother also fried sausage cakes, about two thirds done, put them in three pound lard pails or in quart jars. She then would pour some of the grease, liquid drippings, over the sausage, seal the jar and pail, then turn it upside down. When the grease solidified, she had us to take the sausage to the cellar house, and it would keep for months. We had sausage way up into the spring of the year!

Dad usually slaughtered four to five hogs. He trimmed the hams and shoulders and smoked them in the smoke house for days. The wood he used for smoking the meat was hickory. It had a distinct flavor to it that we enjoyed. He salted the sides of the hog and stored them on tables in the smoke house. This was used for bacon and other cooking. The smoking flavored the meat and kept it from spoiling. We usually kept a ham or two and two or three shoulders for our consumption. Later, when the hams and shoulders were well smoked, dad would trade some of them to the General Store for goods that we needed at home. These items could consist of salt, spices, brown and white beans, sugar, flavorings, flour and other necessary items. Dad would take corn to the mill to have it ground for our cornmeal.

In the cellar, on one side of the room, was a large bin that we stored potatoes in that we used for the winter months. Dad also stored bushels of potatoes in a field nearby that would be used in the springtime. He made a round circle on the ground and put soil about one foot high in this circle. He cupped the soil out slightly then put straw on it. Then he stacked the potatoes up into a large mound, putting a lot of straw over the potatoes, then adding roofing paper. Then he put about two feet of soil on top of the potatoes and they kept all winter. In the spring, we would dig a small hole in the side of the mound and remove potatoes to eat.

We had apple trees and some of them, including peach trees were located on a farm nearby that had been given to dad's brother, uncle Henry, by grand father Williams. We stored apples in the cool cellar and they kept until the first of the year. Mother also prepared apples for frying. She pealed the apple, cut the quarters into two parts, then put a pan full in the bottom of a wooden barrel. She set a saucer with sulphur on top of the apples, lit the sulphur with a match and covered the barrel with a clean towel and a heavy quilt. She kept the apples covered for one day and would repeat the process until the barrel was about two thirds full. Later on in the winter, she would remove some apples, wash them very good and fry them for breakfast. With the breakfast would be hot biscuits, ham, bacon, and sausage, eggs, gravy, jellies, and honey.

The sulphur helped to preserve the apples in the barrel. In later years when I majored in Biology at college, we studied how sulfa drugs were developed and their importance in preventing illnesses. I often wondered about the few colds that we had as youngsters, if the sulphur that was used to preserve the apples, had anything to do with this.

We raised corn and beans to eat in the summer as well as can for use during the winter months. Sometimes, we planted beans along with the rows of corn and the beans would climb the stalk of corn. We would go along and pick the mature beans from their hanging onto the stalk of corn. Mother always canned many quarts and half gallons of beans as well as corn. She also prepared a type of bean that the family really liked. She broke the beans into pieces after stringing them, put them on a white sheet and placed this on a roof of a building for the sunlight to slowly dry out. The sun would remove a high percentage of the moisture from the beans. If she had a bushel of beans on the sheet, it usually ended up as about one peck as all of the moisture had been removed. These "shuck" beans were stored in large covered cans to prevent any moisture from getting into them. In the winter mother would cook about two thirds of a quart, flavoring them with meat from the smoke house, and this made a large kettle of "shuck" beans to eat. What a tasty vegetable to have with other items for dinner.

Cabbage was another vegetable that was utilized very much on the farm. Mother would cook this, flavored with ham, for dinner. She also made slaw from the cabbage. Another item she made from cabbage was kraut. She had an old kraut cutter, which consisted of three blades on a base, with two sides that had a small wooden box that fitted into groves. She would place this over a wooden barrel, and we would help push the cabbage heads over the blades. It cut the cabbage into fine stringy pieces, going into the barrel. Mother would put some coarse salt on the layers of cabbage that had been cut in the barrel. An item that she also put in the barrel was the center stalk of the cabbage head. Later on when the kraut had "set up" forming a salty brine, mother would remove some kraut for dinner and we children almost fought to see who could get the center stalk of cabbage to eat. She usually always divided the stalks equally for us.

In the summer we had blackberries and "huckel berries" to pick. The hukel berries were similar to a blue berry. We would go out on the farm and pick buckets full of black berries. Mother would can many of these as well as make blackberry jelly and blackberry jam. She made a wonderful cake from the blackberry jam. We always had a large grape harbor. Mother would make grape jelly and she would use about two cups of really ripe grapes and put them in a one half gallon jar and pour boiling water over them, seal them, and later on we had a very good grape drink.

We heated our house with wood and cooked with wood. Before the house burned in 1936, we had a fireplace and would put logs on it during the winter nights. If the fire went out by morning, we had to go out to the storage box on the back porch and bring in kindling and small pieces of wood to start a new fire. The kindling came from chestnut trees that had died from a blight some years before. This was a light wood that was very easy to start a fire with. To assist with starting the fire, we also had pine knots. On a large hill on the farm, there had been pine trees that had died and fell to the ground. The trees had decayed, leaving the knotty area where the limb had been attached to the main part of the tree. This "pine knot" was very high in pine resin and was ideal for starting a fire. My brother and I loved going to the hills, looking under the underbrush and decayed leaves, for these "pine knots". We carried them back to the house in a burlap bag.

I recall when I turned six years old, father said I'm giving you this milk cow to take care of. This included throwing hay down to her in the barn as well as milking her in the morning and in the evening. I had already learned to milk, thinking it was a "big deal" when I was five years old

I also assisted with gathering the corn and hay in for storage for the winter. We had a barn that consisted of two barn lofts, where we stored the hay. We had a large crib where we stored the corn that had been shucked from the shocks of fodder in the fields. We usually had a couple of "barn cats" that helped to take care of the mice that got into the corn crib.

An item that was raised on the farm, that we were not allowed to consume, was tobacco. This crop was raised to get some extra money, usually for the holiday season.

The tobacco grew on stalks, the stalks were cut, put on tobacco sticks by a sharp metal item used to permit it to go through the stalk. After about six or eight stalks were put on the tobacco stick, the stick was left in the ground and another stick was filled. The tobacco had matured and when the field was cut, it was hauled to the barn. There were many poles laying horizontally, about four feet apart, in the upper open area of the barn. The tobacco would be on about four and one-half foot sticks on these poles in the barn. There were openings on the side of the barn, in which hinges were attached to a board that run from the top of the barn to about eight feet from the ground. These were opened during the hot weather and it assisted in the tobacco maturing, (curing) properly.

I can vividly recall how my mother helped to strip the tobacco leaves from the stalk, tying about fifteen leaves together forming a "hand of tobacco". These "hands of tobacco" were put on a large square wooden pallet, and another wooden pallet put on top of them and weighted down with heavy weights. This compressed the tobacco together and made it easier to take to the tobacco market to be auctioned.

We were to never use any of this tobacco! I recall one winter, in our new house, with a large heating stove in the living room, I thought I would act like an older brother whom I had observed using tobacco. I got a tobacco leaf and tried to make a cigarette and smoke it. I felt very woozy and laid down on the floor behind the wood heating stove. I got very sick and mother asked me what was wrong and I said I wasn't sure. I ended up going outside and vomiting.

There were many activities on the farm to have fun. One was playing tag in the two loft barn. The poles that went across the rafters were used to hang the tobacco on to cure. We would scramble across these poles playing tag on a rainy day with other boys from the neighborhood. If mother knew we were climbing high up in the barn she would never have let us play there again.

Another activity was sailing small boats in the creek after a large rain. The small boats were carved out of pieces of mature corn stalks. There was a foot log, a tree hewed flat on one side, laying across the creek to get over to the barn. Alongside this foot log was a barb wire fence. Once when my brother Kenneth and I went to play, after a large rain, I started walking across the foot log and the swirling water got me dizzy and I fell onto the fence, cutting a large gash under my upper arm. I then fell into the water, screaming and crying, washing about fifty feet away in a curve of the creek. I jumped out of the water and we went to the house. Mother bandaged the cut after putting turpentine on it, it burned like ?@#, and I was grounded from playing in the creek for quite awhile. I have this long scar today under my upper left arm!

Before we moved to West Virginia, in 1942, a man by the name of Pyle from Morehead, KY came to our house and wanted to drill a gas well. He gave dad $25.00 and if he struck gas, he would provide free gas to the farm. He ended up striking gas. When he struck the gas, they lit the gas and it made a large flame burning in the air. Neighbors came by to see this "big event", prior to his "capping" the well. He stored the large drilling rig in our barn and was planning to drill another well.

When something like this happens, there are those who are not comfortable with the success that a neighbor may be having. The truck that was stored in the barn had been damaged. Someone had slipped into the barn at night and drove nails into the large tires on the truck. Mr. Pyle had to get all of the tires patched prior to moving the truck to another drilling area on the farm as dad had permitted him to drill another well. We moved in April 1942 to West Virginia and I visited back at the old home place in 1946 and they were using gas for heating and cooking.

What a wonderful time a youngster had growing up on a farm like this. There were always chores to do to keep one busy, which taught responsibility. I am grateful that I had these experiences.

# Chapter 8

## MOVING FROM THE SECURE LIFE ON THE FARM
## AND ATTENDING LARGE SCHOOLS

In 1942, the last of April, work began for the packing of the household items that would be moved to a house in West Virginia. I had spent nine wonderful years on the farm and felt sad about moving. Mother had told dad that she wanted to get the younger children, four of us, near schools for an opportunity for an education and also closer to where he worked. He worked for the Chesapeake and Ohio Railway out of Huntington, West Virginia. Most of the time this was on route ten, near the Guyandott River toward Logan WV.

I remember the truck was very large. Dad was in West Virginia and mother and the two girls left with the first load. My brother and I stayed at a neighbor's house and the truck came back the next day. Most of the items were farm implements and other heavy items, a horse and two cows. We went 18 miles to Route 60, a concrete road, near Morhead, on east through Ashland, KY, on through Huntington, WV, turning onto Route 10 South to Pleasant View, WV. I can remember hearing the cows mooing a few times. I couldn't believe the size of the big cities we passed through, Ashland, Ky and Huntington, WV.

When we got to our house in West Virginia, I couldn't believe that there was a high school across the cement road from our house and there was a restaurant near the high school. This was a much different environment than the one we had moved from. We settled into our new surroundings and began adjusting to having neighbors throughout the community. We were not permitted to cross the highway to go over to the high school in the evenings to play for a few months.

In September of 1942, I rode a bus four miles to West Hamlin Grade School. In 1945, when I was in the seventh grade, I joined the Lincoln County Band. The band was composed of three high schools and we would go to Hamlin, the county seat on Saturdays to practice with Hamlin HS and Duval HS. I attended the eighth grade in a building next to the library at the Guyan Valley HS, across the road, (Route 10), from our house.

In 1947 I started to Guyan Valley HS in the ninth grade. The school was located in Pleasant View, WV, across the road from our house, but the address was Rt. 1, Branchland, WV.  I was in the band, played basketball, school plays, yearbook staff, National Honor Society, and played baseball. During my junior year I started dating Carole Cremeans. I remember she gave me a birthday party at her house on December 24 that year. What a wonderful high school time I experienced in those four years.

In the fall of 1951, I started to Marshall College in Huntington, West Virginia. The enrollment was 3100 students. I was in the Marshall College Marching Band, playing the drums. Dr O'Connell was our band director. We participated at Fairfield Stadium for the home football games. After one semester I left for lack of funds, worked some time for the C & O Railway, got laid off and joined the Air Force.

In January 1956, I started back to Marshall College. I graduated in the summer of 1958 with an AB degree in Biological Science and Physical Education. Our graduation exercises were held in the Keith Albee Theater in Huntington. This building is now a Historic Building and has the Marshall University Artists Series there. My wife, my mother and two sisters were there for my graduation. I am the first one to graduate from college. I started teaching and coaching in the fall of 1958 and continued to work on my masters degree.

In January 1961, I received my Masters Degree in School Administration from Marshall University. This was the first graduating class to receive their degree after Marshall became a University.

In the summer of 1962, I attended a 10 week Molecular Biology Institute at Ball State Teachers College (now University), at Muncie Indiana. I did Post Graduate work at Ohio University, at Athens, Ohio, Morhead University, at Morhead, KY, and Vanderbelt University at Nashville, TN. I also took work at Rio Grande University, at Rio Grande, Ohio

# Chapter 9

## HOLIDAYS AND BIRTHDAYS

One of the special holidays for me was Christmas. I was born on this day in 1932 and can say it has been a very festive time as long as I can remember. This was always a time for a celebration in our home. The meaning of Christmas was always emphasized, however my birthday was always celebrated. Mother always had a cake for me and this has continued with my family. My wife has always had a cake for me and she is always reminded by our sons not to forget dad's birthday cake!!

Our stockings were hung above the fireplace in Kentucky and in West Virginia. This continued until we were in high school. Our parents always emphasized the true meaning of Christmas and had lots of food and fruits. Presents were not emphasized so much but we usually got one or two.

Thanksgiving was another holiday that was always celebrated at our house. In the early years mom always had a turkey , ham, sweet potatoes, mashed potatoes, dumplings, corn, beans, beets, pickles, jams and jellies, dressing, nuts, on and on. She continued to do this throughout the years until she could no longer prepare large dinners.

Another important holiday that we always celebrated was Easter. We attended church and had Easter egg hunts in our yard. Mother always participated in these activities. Here again we were instructed as to the meaning of Easter, that our savior arose on Easter Morning. Attending church and Sunday school was always important at our house.

# Chapter 10

## FAILURE AND HOPE

I never gave much thought to failure. We were always taught, if you don't succeed, try again. The work ethic was taught us at an early age, "you must do your best and your best will always do." There were many farm chores to accomplish which taught us the importance of being responsible.

Coming from a religious family, it was instilled in the children that what we had, came from God. Many times I had difficulty understanding this, however I didn't question this belief. We were always told that we lived in the greatest country in the world and if we hoped for the best, eventually we would have the best. There was always a positive attitude in our home, especially from mother. I recall a story from father and mother. Dad would store the potatoes we harvested in a large bin in the cellar. He told mother to use the smallest potatoes first. Mother didn't agree with this and said I will always use the largest potatoes first and I will always have the largest potatoes in the bin to pick from!

We did not have guidance counselors in our school. At an early age I hoped that some day I would become a teacher of young people. I had the highest regard for the teachers I had in school and wanted to someday be like them. In 1958 I became a teacher that I had al always dreamed about and a basketball coach too!

Failure didn't seem to be a part of the vocabulary of our family. It seemed that being positive was always emphasized and happiness should be present each day with us. Mother said happiness is a state of mind and it is up to you to have a positive attitude that enables you to be encouraging to all around you. She always said, "you must never think you are better than someone else, but you must always feel that you are as good as anyone".

# Chapter 11

## TEACHING, COACHING AND HIGH SCHOOL PRINCIPAL

I must say that getting a teaching degree from college was a happy time for Gloria and I. We were living in Huntington during the summer of 1958 and she traveled with me for interviews. On our way back from an interview at Beavercreek, Ohio, we stopped at the Court House at Ironton, Ohio. The County Superintendent's Office was located there. Decatur-Washington School District was looking for a basketball coach and Biology and Science teacher. Mr. Carlton Davidson, the Executive Head of the district drove Gloria and I out to Blackfork, Ohio & showed us the facilities. I accepted the job and started teaching the first of September.

I taught for one week and on Saturday our twin sons were born in Huntington, WV. I had already moved to Oak Hill and was looking forward for Gloria and the children to be coming soon.

I started four black boys on the starting five and we had a very good team. One of the most talented boys that

41

I ever coached was a senior that first year of my coaching. We won ten and lost eight games, but it was a very good season. The students and parents were tremendous individuals.

I had taught and coached for two years at Decatur-Washington H.S. and was hired in the Oak Hill School system as a Jr. High Science and Math teacher and Jr. High Football and Basketball Coach. I taught and coached for two years at this level and assisted in the Varsity program with scouting. Paul Jones, who assisted me in the Jr. Hi program, went with me on scouting trips. The coaching staff in 1961 was myself, Head Coach Len Hellyer, Paul McMillian, Harley Duvall and Bill Haydon.

I served as the Senior Play sponsor and the Jr. Play sponsor in the spring of 1962. Members of the Sr. Play Cast were, Eileen Dunn, Joyce York, Johanna Edwards, Janet Herbert, Brenda Gray, Clyde Whitlatch, Tom Addis, Morgan Jones, Mike Silvey and Bill Parker. The Jr Play cast members were, Jane Evans, Carol McFann, Jean Crusan, Betty Miller, Rita Schaffer, Nancy Davis, Deloris Donley, Sharon Bates, Jennie Roberts, Mary Wiles, Darrell McFann, Dwight Woods, Danny Evans, Jerry Myers, and Greg Wilson. This was certainly a group of outstanding students.

I assisted the Senior Sponsor with the chaperoning of the Senior Trip to Washington DC.

This was a fun time for all participants however we had certain rules that we expected the young adults to comply with. I was in charge of checking the boys rooms on their floor at 12:00 AM to see that all were in their rooms. After checking all rooms, I went back to my room and waited for about forty five minutes and went down to the lobby to check things out. There was a large gathering room that had games and music playing. "Low and behold some one broke the glass on a pin-ball machine", there was Jimmy Waylon, one of our athletes. I checked with the management and we got things worked out and those with Jimmy apologized and went to their room. By the way, Jimmy graduated from college and he earned a Doctors degree!

During the summer of 1962, I was hired at the varsity basketball coach at Oak Hill High School. I taught Biology, Zoology and General Science. The basketball players I had on the team were Danny Brisker, Robert Hall, Mickey James, Mike Foster, Joe Spurlock, Bill Parks, Butch Reese, Frank Elcess and Danny Evans. These students were a great group to work with. Coach Todd Fugate, originally from Milton WV, and a graduate of Marshall College, was the Reserve basketball coach.

I had the opportunity to serve as the Senior High Student Council advisor during 1962-63. The students were: Russell Stiverson, Ricky Davis, Paula Morgan, Connie Evans, Nancy Simpson, Sharon Evans, Mike Evans, Chester Willis, Marsha Wilson, Sharon Bastes, Merrill Detty, Danny Evans, Pat Bates, Carol McFann, and Marcia Wasmer. The Jr. High Council members were: Billy Copas, Tom McNerlin, Dana Rose, Gary Thomas, Roger Williams, Connie Kelly, Becky Brisker and Nancy Gray.

In 1962, Len Hellyer was the head football coach, assisted by Todd Fugate and Tom Kalinoski. The Captain of the team was Greg Wilson. Frank Elcess and Joe Spurlock were Co-Captains. Four seniors on that team were Phil Bowman, Greg Wilson, Jessie Taylor and

Doug Crabtree. Four players who did a lot for the team and were called "the Four Horses", were Greg Wilson, Joe Spurlock, Mickey James and Greg Howell. What a pleasure it was to be associated with such fine young men that gave so much for their school. We tied for the Ohio Valley Conference Championship the 1962 year. Coach Hellyer issued gold pendant footballs, "OVC 1962 Co-Champs" to all involved. I still have one today.

I was teaching a Biology class during the summer of 1963 and was leaving the building and the Superintendent, Mr. Daugherty, called me to his office. He said he had taken another job and Mr. Smith, the principal was taking his job. He asked me if I would be interested in being High School principal. I told him I was interested and he said if he presented my name to the Board of Education that evening did I think I could do the job. I told him, yes sir, I feel capable of doing the job. Mr Daugherty said, "if you told me that you had to go home and ask your wife what she thought, I would open the job up and have interviews". I was appointed high school principal that night at the Board of Education meeting.

The beginning of the 1963 school year was a terrific time in my life. Getting everything organized for the opening of school was an enjoyable task. Making the schedule for the teachers, assigning them to classrooms, checking class lists, receipting and marking textbooks. A difficult task for me was carrying the textbooks, used and new, from the storage room to the classrooms. I checked all equipment orders in during the summer and located it in the classrooms. I was also responsible for the scheduling of all athletic events and contracting of the officials and attending the athletic contests.

I had been elected a delegate to represent our school system at the Ohio Education Association meeting that fall in Columbus, Ohio. I will never forget sitting in the Veterans Memorial Auditorium, and an individual came to the microphone and said, "all meetings are cancelled, the President of the United States has been killed". I came home and my wife, children and I went to my mother's house and we observed on television the killing by Jack Ruby of Oswald. Many thought Ruby was involved in some way with the killing of the President.

Our twin sons played football, basketball and track. Tim and Jon were on the basketball team in 1976 that ranked third in the state of Ohio in the Associated Press poll. They each were in the State track meet at Ohio State Football stadium in Columbus, Ohio. Tim was in the 880 yard relay and Jon was in the high jump. Tim got Woody Hayes', football coach of Ohio State, signature on a program book that he still has. Todd made the all-state basketball team in division IV and played in Canton Ohio his senior year. I enjoyed all the athletics in our school and especially our son's participation.

Our twin sons, Tim and Jon graduated in 1977 and Todd graduated in 1981.

# Chapter 12

## ILLNESSES AND REMEDIES

I had few illnesses as a child. I recall that I would get what mother called the "kroup". She had a remedy in which she put camphor on my chest and neck and would put hot cloths on it. I hated the smell of the camphor. I recall another remedy that mother had was castor oil. I thought she utilized this too much when we were youngsters. Another illness was a very sore throat. Now days the doctor would say you have the strep throat. Mother would roll a sheet of paper up, put some sulphur in the roll and blow it back into my throat. This was a harrowing experience, however it usually cleared the sore throat up.

It is interesting that when I went to college and was studying Biology, I learned that sulfa drugs were developed that helped strep throat. I suppose some of the home remedies that were used years ago did some good.

I think the year was 1944. I recall it was during the summer as we had to mow the lawn with a push lawn mower. My brother Kenneth and I mowed our very large lawn. We trimmed the edges and surrounding areas with a sickle. The sickle had been left in the yard, near the corner of the house. I came running barefooted around the house and my foot hit the sickle. It made a large slash on my foot and did I scream! I hobbled to the back of the house crying and screaming. Mother saw I was cut and she always kept white cloths for situations like this. Mother quickly washed the cut, laying the part that had been cut back on the foot then pouring turpentine on it. This hurt more than the cut! She bandaged the foot and I was out of commission for a few days.

When I went into the Air Force in 1952, I was in basic training at Sampson Air Force Base in Geneva, New York. Every week our squadron had duty to do at different places on the base. I received duty at the freezers where they stored frozen meats for the mess halls. We went into the refrigerated box cars on the railroad tracks and took the sides of frozen beef into the freezers. This would be all day long. The weather was extremely hot and we went into the freezers to store the beef. t was after this that I began experiencing swelling in my feet with much pain in the joints. I wanted to stay with the men in our squadron and graduate with them.

We attended classes during the day and after sitting for quite awhile, I had difficulty getting up and walking without it showing that I was in much pain. When I got up of the morning I could hardly walk and my ankles were swelling so large that I could hardly get my shoes on. I had to leave them unlaced and hardly tied. The First Sargent came to my bed one late evening and said I realize you want to stay with the men in your squadron, however you must go to the hospital and be treated and if you do not loose more that five days, you will be returned back to your unit.

I went to the hospital in an ambulance and after seven days there, the Sargent sent my clothes in my duffle bag. I stayed in the hospital for 143 days with rheumatic fever. I developed a heart mummer as a result of this.

My mother, my oldest sister, Ida Mae, and her husband, Scott came to see me once while I was in the hospital. What an experience. I returned to another squadron and finished my basic training. I then went home on leave and went to Cheyenne, Wyoming for training in supply school. I was sent then to Alaska for fifteen months and then back to Reno, Nevada.

When I was discharged from the Air Force, they listed me as less than ten percent disabled. This was because I had contracted rheumatic fever in the service. I was listed as a disabled American Veteran.

I was out of the Air Force for about ten years and applied for veterans compensation and they refused it and said I could appeal the decision. I did not appeal.

I was talking to Joe David a retired Air Force person in 1999 and told him about the experience I had of getting a heart mummer in the Air Force and he encouraged me to reapply for veterans compensation. I did reapply in 2003, they refused it and said I could appeal, which I did. I had forgot all about the application and Gloria and I arrived from Myrtle Beach in January 2005, where we were living for three months. A check for two years back pay was received in the mail. The application had been approved and I was listed as 10 percent disabled. I now receive a small monthly check from the Government.

My brother Kenneth, in Ft. Lauderdale, FL., said I should have hounded those rascals continually as they had an obligation to take care of this incident and should have been paying since 1955. He had been wounded in the Marine Corps in Korea in 1953.

# Chapter 13

## RELIGION

## "Hell and the Stovepipe"and "Mike the Monkey"

At a very early age I realized that my mother and father placed a great emphasis upon relying on a higher power to help us. Mom always had bedtime prayers with us children and had us to repeat, "Now I lay me down to sleep, I pray the Lord my soul to keep, and if I die before I awake, I pray the Lord my soul to take". She explained to us about going to a wonderful place when we died and we did not need to fear this. She taught us that God would take care of us and everything we had came from God. Mother read and explained the Bible to us as children. As a very young child I heard preachers preach about going to hell, and if you didn't live a Christ like life, you could burn in hell, really scary talk for very young child!

There wasn't an organized denomination in this rural area. Usually traveling preachers would come to the area and have revivals in the one room school house. They always rode a horse, as I remember, as there were very few cars in this area..

When I was about four years old, in Kentucky, mother took us children to a  revival meeting that was being held in the one room schoolhouse. Kerosene lamps hung on the walls of the room and a large potbelly stove was in the middle of the room with the stove pipe going through the top of the ceiling. It was very common for some churchgoers to get happy and start shouting. Mother laid me in the seat of a school desk near the stove to keep warm. I went to sleep and was awaken by a large noise, looking up, I saw sparks a flying with some smoke, and I thought, "Oh my Lord, this must be hell a coming." Mother came running and carried me to the back of the room. Some of the men put gloves on and reassembled the stove pipes for the smoke to get out properly and church was continued. My mother told me later that Bill Watson, who wore gum boots, got happy, started shouting, throwing his arms and going from one side of the room to the other and hit the stove pipe with his arms and knocked them down. This actually happened - what an experience!

When we moved to West Virginia, mother and dad took us to Sunday School and to church.  At least once a year,  a revival meeting was held in our church. We would go sometime to other churches that were holding revival meetings at a different time. The building we used for our church was located in a large room in the back of the Bethlehem Tabernacle. This tabernacle had been erected by the United Baptist Association. This was an association of Baptist Churches throughout the region. In 1954, the people of the church organized a building committee and built a new church. My mother and father were original members of this church.

I have always maintained that religion is an important part of an individual's life. Mother instilled this in us.

How does a story of a monkey get related to those attending the Convention of the Association of United Baptist's at the Bethlehem Tabernacle there in Pleasant View? After World War II ended, John Midkiff, a C & O Railway small station agent, at Branchland, WV. came to our house, knocked on the door and mother answered the door. He said Mrs. Williams, I have a shipment for you up at the station and you can pick it up in the morning. He said it is a monkey and I gave it water and a banana for tonight. She said where did it come from? I didn't order it. He said it is from New York and the person that sent it is George T. Williams.

My oldest brother George, who was in the Merchant Marines, had docked in New York. They were bringing quite a few cages of Rhesus monkeys back on this boat. The monkeys were to be used for medical research. Before the boat docked, some of the sailors let a couple of cages of the monkeys loose. A call came out for volunteers to help catch them. They were told they would get something for assisting with catching the monkeys. All of the men selected cigarets or Wrigleys Spearmint gum. My brother said he told an officer that he would help if they gave him a monkey. This they did and he sent the monkey home to my brother and I..

We named him Mike and built a tall cage in the plum orchard located on the elevated bank lying behind our house. Before we constructed the cage, we put Mike in a bedroom which had shades and curtains over the windows and left food and water for him. Mike tore the curtains to shreds and the shades received the same treatment.

There were many United Baptist Churches throughout this area and they held their annual convention in their tabernacle across the road, which was about one hundred yards from the high school. Each summer during this three day convention, people would come from many, many miles to these services. They had preaching, singing and also some business was taken care of. There were food booths with cold drinks, watermelon, green beans, cole slaw, potatoes, cornbread, corn on the cob, sandwiches - some of which were mutton. The sheep were slaughtered near the river for these sandwiches. What an experience, going near the river and seeing them slaughter the sheep!

My brother and I had an idea that these churchgoing people would pay to see Mike the Monkey at the William's house. We put signs up, "See Mike the Monkey" - 10 cents.

Our house was just across the road from the high school. About 70 cars used the area around the high school and near the tabernacle to park their automobiles. People began to come up the bank, through the yard next to the side of the house and on up in the plum orchard where the cage was located. If we only had a video recorder in those days, what recordings we would have!

The people were amazed and startled that they had experienced seeing a monkey. Mike would swing on his swing, going from side to side, jump upon two shelves we had in the cage and make faces at the onlookers as well as a crazy screech when people yelled at him. Our first summer, we made $122.00.

We kept Mike for another summer and cut the price to five cents and we made $48.00. Our mother called George who was working in Cincinnati, Ohio and told him to come and get Mike. We didn't want to continue with the work required to keep him. George came and took Mike and gave him to the Cincinnati Zoo. This little business deal had to be told here as it relates to an enterprise by two youngsters helping churchgoers have fun as well as their duty to attend the church services at the tabernacle.

I drifted away from attending church during the armed forces and during college. When I got my first job teaching and coaching in 1958, Rev. Gregory, Margil McFann & Martha Detty, visited our house quite regular. We had twin boys and they invited the family to church. I was so busy at that time that I very seldom saw them, however my wife started going to the Evangelical United Brethren Church in Oak Hill, Ohio. She was asked by Rev. Gregory, how often does you husband make it home? I was gone for many long hours a day taking care of my coaching responsibilities.

In the fall of 1965, I had the experience of accepting Jesus Christ as my personal savior and was baptized by Rev. Harold Sturm. This instilled in me the importance to try always to do what was right and to show love and respect to our family and others.

I have served as lay leader, Sunday School Superintendent, Chairman of Pastor Relations Committee in our church. I have been a certified Lay Speaker of The United Methodist Church and a participant in Lay

Witness Missions in Ohio and other states. Religion is an integral part of our family.

# Chapter 14

## PROPERTY MY PARENTS OWNED
## WHAT I OWNED

My father's farm in Tippet, KY was given to him by his father. There were three other adjoining farms of 160 acres that grandfather Williams gave to three other children. Aunt Mizalphia, Aunt Martha and Uncle Henry. Grandfather left about an acre of land on the farm that he gave dad for a Williams Cemetery, which continues to be in operation today. I have some of the records from the Rowan County Court House of the finalization of the deed for dad's farm.

In 1941, mother was wanting dad to move the family out of the hollow where we lived. She said it would be so much better if he obtained a place in West Virginia, nearer to where he worked for the Chesapeake and Ohio Railroad. He worked out of the Huntington C & O Division and most of his locations were between Huntington and Logan West Virginia, on the railroad that was parallel to the Guyandott River. He was a cook, living in railroad cars, which were called camp cars. The workers lived in these railroad cars during the week. These camp cars would be placed on a railroad siding, along the railroad tracks. These workers would be moved to another area on the division of the railway system when they completed working in an area.

Mother said the most important reason that she wanted dad to move was to give the four youngest children an opportunity for an education. We went to a one room school and if we went to high school, dad would have had to pay room and board for us to go to Morhead High School. None of the other children had gone, except our oldest brother George who went to Normal School in 1929 long enough to qualify to teach in the Hardyman one room school.

In the spring of 1942, dad bought a 73 acre hillside farm in Pleasant View, WV, across the paved road in front of the Guyan Valley High School. I credit my mother with her persistence for dad to move us from the hollow, that I had the opportunity for and education. I shall always be so thankful for her insight into the importance of an education. Three of us graduated from high school, two attended college with me graduating from college with an AB and MA degree.

In 1965, six years after obtaining my first teaching job, we built a new split level house, on .48 acre, just outside the corporation limits of Oak Hill, Ohio. Our twin boys were six years old at this time and our youngest son was 2 ½ years old. This was our home from 1965 until June 2006.

In May 2006 we sold our house in Oak Hill and came to North Carolina. We lived with our youngest son, Todd, his wife and child until our house was completed.

We moved into our  house in South Carolina, Indian Land, Sun City Carolina Lakes October 2, 2006.  This is a Dell Web Community.

# Chapter 15

## DID I REMEMBER THE DEPRESSION?
## A $5.00 BILL IN A PINT JAR

Being born in 1932, I had no knowledge of the hardships of the previous years. I do remember that the house we lived in, that had been given to my father by his dad, burned to the ground. My sister, Lorena, who was thirteen at the time, told me in later years that this occurred December 5, 1936 and that mother had gone to Morhead, Ky. to do some shopping.

This was a memorable time in my life. Dad hired Mr Plank, who owned a sawmill to cut lumber from trees on the farm for a house. He stored it during the winter and had Ray Clark, a carpenter to start building in the spring of the year.

Dad rented an old house near Aunt Mizalphia's old home place, just up the road from the graveyard on our farm. The house was built on a bank near the side of a dirt road, with large timbers underneath the back side of it to hold it up. I remember mom getting cardboard and nailing to the walls, covering the cracks, and covering this with old newspapers and then using wallpaper. I remember that we had a large garden and neighbor women would come to our house and help mother can vegetable. An interesting experience was once when they came to help string bushels of green beans to can, they all seemed to be so friendly and helpful.

My brother, Kenneth who was about a year and one-half older than I, and I had heard mom and dad talk before about going to the bank. They said they had some money in it and if they left it a certain length of time it would grow into more! We had never been to the town of Morhead and we didn't understand what they were actually talking about. We didn't have any knowledge about the bank or what they were talking about!

My oldest brother George, was working in Cincinnati, Ohio and he sent mother a five dollar bill. Kenneth and I saw it on a small dresser one day and we took it, tore it into small squares and put it into a pint canning jar and put a lid on it. We took the jar under the backside of the house on the bank where the timbers were supporting the house and buried it in "the bank".

Later we heard mother saying she couldn't find the $5.00 dollar bill. She looked and looked and asked us if we had seen it. She was almost in tears and Kenneth and I said mom we know where it is. She said thank goodness boys let me have it as I need to pay for some things. We took her around back, under the house and dug up the jar and told her we put into the bank for it to grow and make more money! She began to cry, boys I don't know if I can spend this now that you have torn the bill up.

Mother was a good seamstress as she made our shirts and much of the clothing that we wore. She took a small needle and thread and sewed the pieces of the bill together. She said she was going to take it to Morhead Citizens Bank and see if they could do anything to help her. Later she took the five dollar bill to the bank.

She told us later that she took the bill to the bank and went in to the cashier and showed it to her and asked her if they could help her. The lady said what in the world happened to the bill? She explained what her four and five year old boys had done to try and help the family. The bank knew that our house had burned and we were trying to build again. She said Mrs. Williams, I want the bank president to hear this story, called him out of his office and mother told it to him. He just laughed and said he had never heard of something like this happening and they gave her another $5.00 bill. Mother came home so excited that everything was alright and hugged us and said we were wonderful boys.

# Chapter 16

## OUR CHILDREN

Gloria and I lived at 1229 ½ sixth avenue in Huntington, West Virginia from May 1956 through the summer of 1958. This was just about one half block from the Chesapeake and Potomac Telephone Company where she worked as an operator when I was going to Marshall College. I graduated from Marshall in July 1958.

The last of August, I had an older brother Loren, to help me move to an apartment in Oak Hill, Ohio as I had got a job to start in September at Decatur-Washington High School at Blackfork, Ohio. Gloria stayed with her mother this short period of time. I came on to Oak Hill and started my first week of teaching, and on Friday afternoon of that first week, the principal, Mrs Eva D. Caulley, came to my room and said your wife has been taken to Cabell Huntington Hospital and I know you are looking forward for a new child. I left school and went to the hospital.

I must tell an interesting story about Gloria's doctor. Dr. Wayburn was an outstanding doctor in Huntington and I would go with her sometimes on her doctor's visit. I would kid him and tell him that I didn't think I would pay him if it wasn't a boy. I arrived at the hospital Friday evening and it wasn't until around noon Saturday that she delivered. I was very tired and the nurse came to the waiting room and said I will call you in just a couple of minutes. She came and told me to come with her and took me to the hallway where Gloria was on a bed with a child in one arm and Dr Wayburn said, it's a girl. I said thank goodness and started to leave for a phone and he took me by the shoulder and pulled the sheet back from another baby and said two girls. I was so excited I yelled, how great, twin girls, I have to run to the phone. Dr. Wayburn pointed and said, look more closely, twin boys. I almost passed out! Dr. Wayburn said I needed to get you back for your always kidding me when you came with Gloria for her doctors visit's. Gloria said the next day, Dr. Wayburn came into the room and started counting the roses and when he finished at twelve, he said, "young lady, don't start out like this. He is to get you another dozen roses. Dr. Wayburn had never told us she was carrying twins during the pregnancy.

Timothy George Williams, Sep. 5, 1958, his middle name is after my fathers.

Jonathan Denver Williams, Sep. 5, 1958, his middle name is after Gloria's father.

I continued teaching and coaching and I went to a Molecular Biology Institute at Ball State Teachers College in Muncie, Indiana the summer of 1962. Another Biology teacher from Michigan said he would like to run a survey to see how many of us had children nine months after we got home that summer. I finished the Institute near the end of August, came home and we went to Mammoth Cave, in Kentucky for a few days vacation before I went back to teaching. Nine months later our third son was born, Christopher Todd Williams, May 26, 1963.

Timothy married Mary McClellan from Chardon, Ohio and they have four children, Jonathan, Jane, Sarah, and Margaret. Tim and his wife are pharmacists and they own a pharmacy and she works in a hospital.

Jonathan Denver Williams married Cindy Christenson from Carlyle, Iowa and they have three daughters, Bree Ann, Kaylynn, and JenaLee. John started teaching and coaching basketball in Iowa as his father had done many years before. Four years later he started working for an Insurance company and stayed for about twenty years. They downsized the company and he returned to coaching and teaching business and computers. I think this is what he truly loves doing. He just finished his Master Degree and is going into administration. His wife Cindy is a nurse.

Christopher married Tammy Adkins from Oak Hill and they had been married for seventeen years when along came Camryn, their daughter. Todd is in hospital finance and his wife, Tammy, is a pharmacist. They live in Charlotte, NC.

# Chapter 17

## JOBS

You already know that I was born on a farm and if you are somewhat familiar with responsibilities for farm children, you realize that they have chores to do. At a very young age, I helped to hoe in the garden, feed chickens everyday, gather eggs everyday, and feed cattle in the barn. I had been taught how to milk and when I turned six years old, my parents gave me a cow to milk and that was a responsibility I had every day.

In 1942 when we moved to West Virginia there were three neighbors who grazed their milk cows on our farm and would come to the barn to milk every morning and evening. The cows would graze quite some distance away in the fields on our hillside farm. In the evening, my brother and I, and sometimes a friend or two, would be asked to go bring the cows in from grazing so they could milk them. Sometimes we would leave to get the cows and we started playing and become lackadaisical in our duties. I will never forget, a lady that everybody called "Aunt Lizzie", said "when you send one boy to do a job, he will do the job, send two and they will do one half of a job and send three or more and they will do no job at all".

My brother and I plowed our garden and corn fields with our horse. The ladies asked us if we could plow their gardens and we did. Other neighbors asked us to prepare their gardens and we made some extra money doing this in the spring of the year. We could be seen in the spring of the year going to neighbors gardens with the harrow, drag and turning plow on the sled pulled by our horse.

During the summer of 1949, Daily and Daily Pole Line Construction, a small company form Clarksburg, West Virginia, came through our area to replace some of the older telephone poles with new ones and string four new telephone wires on the poles from Huntington to Ranger, W.VA. We lived in a large house and mother roomed and boarded these four men. Kenneth, my older brother and I got a job working for this company. It was our first job in which we received a paycheck. I worked as a labor - helper, and then I learned to climb telephone poles, stringing the new telephone wires. I made 75 cents per hour and some days we worked ten hours a day and sometimes on Saturday. This was a wonderful summer job.

During one week end when the men went back to Clarksburg where they were from, Kenneth and I took one of their large trucks, as we knew where the keys were and went to Huntington at the vegetable and fruit market. This was about twenty five miles away. We bought two bushels of peaches and came back home and slipped them on the back porch and showed them to mom the next morning. We told her that we bought them from Mr.

Adkins, a man who peddled fruit from a truck at a town near by. She was so happy with the fruit and canned all of the peaches except for making a delicious peach cobbler. In later years, we told mom about this episode and she said, "I cant believe you boys did a thing like that".

The next summer, which was1950, Ercil J. Midkiff, a friend of mine and I got a job working for a natural gas pipe line contractor over beyond Hamlin, WV. This was on the other side of Lincoln County where we lived. Our parents packed our lunches and we traveled in Ercils father's 1937 Ford car.

The construction consisted of large bulldozers making a right of way for large ditching machines to make a large ditch for large steel pipes to be welded together and laid in the ditch. This line would carry natural gas. We were labors making $1.00 per hour. This was good money however after about two weeks a union representative was stopping the workers as they went to their cars at the end of the day and said if you sign up for the union and we get fifty one percent of the workers to sign up you will make $1.25 per hour. The owner passed the word that his contract could be broken by him and he would pull out and there would be no jobs if a union was formed. We thought he was bluffing us and we joined the union. Over fifty one percent of the men joined and three and one half weeks later we went to work and all of the machinery was gone and we had no jobs. We learned a tough lesson.

I graduated from high school, Monday evening, May 14, 1951. The next day three high school friends, Jimmy McComas, Kyle Garretson, Kenny Courts and I left on a

Greyhound bus for Detroit, Michigan to get a job in an automobile plant. We were all eighteen years old.

I started to work Thursday from 3:00 PM to 11:00 PM. at Detroit Gear and Axle. I walked to and from work which was about eight blocks away. I received my paycheck on Thursday and was told to take a different way home on paydays, as I would less likely get robbed My job was to put the right and left part of the front bumper, for the 1952 model Chevrolet cars, on an assembly line that sanded these parts. This was preparing the parts to go to another assembly line to go through the chromium vats.

I met a man from Ireland when we ate our lunches. I told him that I planned to work for 90 days and go back home and register for college. He told me that he had been there for many years and he had never seen anyone leave to go back to school. He told his wife about me and she would send me pineapple upside down cake every so often. She told him to keep reminding me to leave after ninety days to go to college and if I didn't she would never send anymore pineapple upside down cake to me. After my ninety days were up, I took a Greyhound bus home to register for college.

I never had any literature on colleges and when I got home I decided that I would go to Montgomery, WV., to register at West Virginia Institute of Technology. I hitch-hiked north on Route 10 to Route 60, near Huntington, then hitch-hiked Rt. 60 to Montgomery and registered for college. I came back home and that week end, Mildred, my older sister who worked at Sylvania Electric in Huntington, came home. She said mom is he really going to college? I told her what I had done. She said to mother, my landlady has a room above me in the two story house that I rent from and he could stay there and eat in my kitchen, bringing vegetables & etc from the farm and go to Marshall College. I decided to stay where my sister lived in Huntington, WV.

I made the long trek, hitch-hiking back to Montgomery, asked for my money back at the registrars office, and got upset that they charged me $5.00 for having to refund it to me. I went to Huntington and registered at Marshall, in the School of Education, as I wanted to become a teacher. The tuition for that semester in the fall of 1951 was $42.50.

I rode two city busses from where I lived, at 339 ½ Adams Avenue, to the college. One afternoon when I got off the second bus, on my way to the house, I had to pass a small drive inn restaurant and a sign was in the window for a grill cook. I went in and talked to the owner and he asked if I could fry hamburgers, cheeseburgers, make hot dogs, barbecue and french fries. I said yes and he asked me if I had any experience and I told him I had worked some at a restaurant during my senior year in high school. He hired me and I worked with a curb girl, who took orders and delivered the food out to the automobiles. This job lasted until about December 15th. I finished the semester of college and went home, as I had no money for second semester.

I got a job working for the Chesapeake & Ohio Railroad at Peach Creek, West Virginia. This was a town about 40 miles south on Route 10 from where we lived. I rode with Ronald Ray's father. Ronald was a friend of mine who had graduated with me from high school. Mr. Ray was an inspector with the oiler and packer group and

I was a labor doing oiling and packing on the coal cars, prior to their being made up into a train, to be taken away from the railroad yard. This job lasted about three months and the company began to lay off quite a few employees.

I joined the Air Force in April and took basic training at Sampson Air Force Base in Geneva, New York. I then came home for a 26 day leave, on to Cheyenne, Wyoming to attend Supply School. After a twenty-eight day leave home, I shipped out of Camp Stoneman, California on The President Jackson ship to Seward, Alaska. I have a copy of the Casual Mess Pass as well as the Compartment Pass for the ship in one of my scrap books. We took a train from Seward to Fairbanks to get our assignment. The food on the train was hamburgers, hot dogs and baked beans prepared on a large coal burning stove. This was a pretty slow ride, as the train had to stop a number of times for elk on the railroad tracks. We had to stop once for a few hours of layover as a mudslide had covered a part of the railroad track.

After I arrived in Fairbanks, we were assigned to Quonset hut type barracks, which were heated with coal stoves. I was there for about three days and received orders that I was assigned to a radar outpost at Galena Alaska, just off the Yukon River. I flew in a C-47 airplane the two hundred fifty miles northwest to Galena. Flying was the only way to get to the outpost. There were radar outposts located in many areas of Alaska. These were used to detect any enemy aircraft that might be coming toward the United States. The United States was very concerned about Russia at that time.

We had many fishing and hunting opportunities while we were there. We would go out with our carbines and our 45's and enjoy the shooting activities. We would camp near our fishing areas and the beavers would keep us awake at night by hitting their tails on the water and making a loud sound. The native Alaskans did not want us to destroy any fish but give them all that we didn't keep. They would dry the fish out on the top of buildings they built for drying fish..

When I was there with the 743rd Aircraft Control and Warning Squadron, I took a test with thirty other Airmen for a higher speciality code in the areas of our responsibility. The highest score that you could receive was 150 points. I scored 145 points and the closest to me was Lyle Larson, a Swede from Minnesota.

When I was sent back to the states, I was stationed in Reno, Nevada at Stead Air Force Base. I was assigned to 364th Air Rescue Squadron. After about four months living on base, they permitted NCO's of higher rank to live off base. I drew subsistence and housing pay during this time.

I was assigned to an Advanced Supply School, Organizational Supply Supervisor, in Cheyenne, Wyoming. I went there and completed the school. Colonel Sutherland, Office of the School Commandant, sent me a letter to personally congratulate me on completing the technical training course and that I had the highest academic standing in my graduating class. As I look back on these experiences, I can only think of what a great time it was doing my work in the Air Force.

I got out of the Air Force in July 1955 and returned to the Chesapeake and Ohio Railway, where I had worked prior to going into service. My seniority had been going on while I was in service.

On August 16, 1955, I bought my first car. It was a 1951 two door, baby blue Ford Custom.

The car was purchased at Gallagher Motor Sales in Huntington, WV. I started my paperwork to receive the G.I. Bill to go back to college. I got all of this processed in October and worked until December 24. I took a leave of absence and started back to Marshall College in January of 1956.

I married Gloria Watson in May 1956 and we lived at 1229 ½ 6th Avenue, Huntington, WV. I worked the summer of 1957 painting a house in Huntington and I helped a company move all of their inventory to another part of town.

Upon graduation in July of 1958, I obtained a job coaching and teaching at Decatur-Washington High School in Lawrence County, Ohio and we lived in Oak Hill, Ohio

After teaching at Decatur Washington High School for two years, I worked for the Oak Hill School System. I taught and coached for five years and then served as high school principal for twenty-two years. After this I served for eleven years as executive assistant. This involved supervisor of in-service for the district, curriculum coordinator, director of special placement of students programs, cafeterias supervisor, and part time elementary principal.

# Chapter 18

## POLITICS

Could it happen today? In May 1956, when I was going to college, a friend of mine asked if I would be interested in hauling voters to the polls, on election day, in the county I was from. I knew we would get a day off from college for election day and I told him I was. He said we would meet the individual who would give us the addresses he had for the voters that we were to pick up and haul to the polls. This individual said we would get paid our gas money and $40.00 for the days work. My friend was also using his car to haul voters.

At about 5:30 P.M., the person that said we would get $40.00, told us that really gas was enough for our services and he felt that we would be helping the party to volunteer our services. I immediately stopped hauling voters and went to my mother's house. My friend, Ralph, who had been helping, had been told the same thing. He came to mother's house about 6:00 P.M. and told me not to worry, that when his dad, who was higher on the political ladder in the party, heard about this, he would take care of it.

About 9:00 P.M. that evening the individual that told us we would get $40.00 for our work, came to the house, apologized for the misunderstanding and gave me my $40.00. Needless to say, after this experience, I never had any aspirations to get involved in the political process.

I am amazed of the corruption that is occurring in our political system today.

# Chapter 19

## YES, I REMEMBER WARS

I had two brothers to serve in WWII. George T, my oldest brother was in the Merchant Marine. I recall when he came home on leave that he always brought something. Once it was a pillow cover with a poem to "Mother" written on it with United States Merchant Marines across the top. This was shortly after he received his basic training. I also recall that he brought a carton of Wrigley Spearmint gum home once as no one was able to get gum at that time.

He traveled in convoys delivering material to other branches of the armed forces. They had to defend themselves on the seas if there were encounters. I recall another time, he had been to Cairo, Egypt and brought back a leather trunk. This was used by me during high school years and after I went into service, someone removed it from mother's house. He also brought a very nice vase from Egypt.

I thought so much of George because of his intellectual ability. When he landed in ports throughout the world, he tried to visit places of cultural interests. He brought coins from other countries and other memorabilia. He said once they had an encounter with a German Mescherschmidt plane and they shot it down, crashing near the port. He was able to get the aluminum nose of this plane and he sent it home. My brother, Cartmal's son-in-law, took this out of my mothers old storage house and took it home.

Cartmal, another brother served during WWII. He was first assigned to the 82$^{nd}$ Airborne Division and later was transferred to the 101$^{st}$ Airborne Division, Glider Section. He was trapped in Bastogne. This was when the German General asked the Americans to surrender and the famous response by General McAullif, the American General was, "NUTS". It took the Germans over four hours to learn the meaning of his response.

I heard many of the stories Cartmal told about being overseas for about four years. I have a book that a Lt. Colonel wrote about this group of men and Cartmal's name is included near the front of the book. Throughout the book there are many pictures of soldiers. Over in the book is a picture of Cartmal and four other soldiers in Germany. The title of this book is "Kilogram".

George came home from the war a few weeks before Cartmal. Mother had dad, George, Cartmal, Loren, Kenneth, my brother at home, and I to go to Huntington and have a picture made. Cartmal wore his Army uniform in this picture. Each of us have this large picture today of the "Williams" men. Tim, our oldest son has the picture.

I will always remember when a brother came home on leave and went to the road, just in front of the house, to catch the Greyhound bus back to camp. Mother always greeted them farewell, always smiling and just as soon as the bus picked him up, mother went into a bedroom and cried and cried.

I have a small glass frame, 5" x 4". It is outlined in red with a square of two blue stars vertically on white. Above the white is a picture of an eagle, as if holding these two stars and the small flag at the bottom with the words "For God and Country". On the reverse side is the following, "As a token of our loyalty and respect to the members of your family who serves in the Armed Forces of America." McBRAYER'S, Morheads Complete Furniture Store, J. Earl McBrayer, Prop. Mr. McBrayer's gave this to mother. Mother always displayed this in a front window of the house, denoting that two from this home were serving in the armed forces. This was very familiar during WWII. Mother gave this memento to me and I will be giving this to our only grandson, Jonathon Williams, as it represents somewhat of a connection with his fathers uncles. It is displayed in my office at home.

I remember the Korean War very vividly. My brother, Kenneth, who I had been in high school with, got injured in this war. He received the Purple Heart. My out of state assignment was with the Air Force was in Alaska.

# Chapter 20

## INFLUENCE OF BOOKS, MUSIC AND MOVIES ON LIFE

At a very early age in life, my mother would always read to the children in the evening. After the chores were completed and supper was over she would gather us around a table and read to us. The lighting in the house was kerosene lamps. Mother always had the lamp shades perfectly clean for a well lighted room. The book that had a great impact on me was the struggles that were encountered in "Uncle Tom's Cabin", by Harriet Beecher Stowe. Mother had ordered this book from Sears and it had been delivered by the postman on horseback. People borrowed this book and mother always told the person to pass it on to others. She had her name in it and said to return it to her but it never was returned. We were the only people up this 18 mile hollow to subscribe for a Sunday newspaper. Mother always wanted to know more about "the outside world". I remember in 1937, I was only four and one-half years old, when the German Airship exploded in New Jersey. Mother read this to us from the Cincinnati Post and showed us the pictures of it.

In 1941, mother took Kenneth, myself and Joyce to Cincinnati, Ohio to visit Ida Mae, our oldest sister. Ida took Kenneth and I to the movie, "Black Beauty". This was my first movie. I vaguely remember much about the movie, however the newsreels they showed about the war really scared me. The planes seemed to be coming directly toward me and I would duck below the seat. What an experience for a country boy!

I wasn't exposed to any music in our home, however, I heard stories in which mom said, dad used to play the mandolin and the fiddle. She said sometime later in her marriage, she felt they shouldn't have string instruments in the home, and she had him to get rid of them. This was a religious belief. We had a radio and listened to the Grand Ole Opry and some neighbors would come to hear it in the late 1930's. We also had a Victrola that played recordings that got burned in the house.

I was interested in musicians and writers when I was in grade school. I have a music book that I made in 1944 at West Hamlin Grade School. One of the pictures in it is of Count Basie, playing the piano.

I joined the Lincoln County Band playing the drums. In 1946 as an eighth grader, I was in the high school band. It was just after the WWII and Louie Hoff was the director. I practiced very much, as the director met us only once a week and we were to turn into him a practice chart the following week that we had practiced one hour a day. I always tried to keep this schedule and did so until I was about a sophomore in high school. Many of the students in band told me you don't have to practice that long, but put that amount of time down on the chart anyway.

I made three All State bands in high school. This was a concert band made up of band members throughout the state of West Virginia. We gave two concerts during our annual West Virginia three day band festival. One of these concerts was held at the City Auditorium. I was asked by a conductor who practiced the all state band if I would introduce the guest conductor from the University of Kentucky at our second concert. All of Lincoln County Band members were present to hear some of their fellow band members perform in this band. There were about 2500 people in attendance, including my mother and an older sister. This was a great experience, leaving the percussion section, coming to the front of the stage to the microphone and saying, "Ladies and gentlemen and fellow band members, I have the pleasure of presenting our guest conductor, from the University of Kentucky, Dr. Frank J. Prindll - Dr. Prindll. He autographed my drum head and I have this memento today.

There were marching bands throughout the state that performed during the three day festival. On Saturday, the last day of the festival, the bands would march from downtown Huntington, out to Fairfield Stadium. The bands would perform a marching presentation on the field and this was a highlight of the festival. We always ranked high on these shows.

The fall of 1951, when I started Marshall College, I enrolled in the marching band. We performed at the home football games for Marshall at Fairfield Stadium.

I was influenced by Louie Hoff, my high school band director as much as any teacher. He was certainly a dedicated and inspiring teacher. I wrote him a letter in later years. This was about two years before he passed away with cancer while living in Portland, Oregon with a son. I told him what an inspiration he had been for me in my life and how much I appreciated him as a person and educator. He wrote a letter back thanking me and I have this letter in one of my scrapbooks.

# Chapter 21

## TURNING POINTS IN MY LIFE

One of the greatest disappointments I recall early in life was when my mother requested my father to move the family out of the"hollow" in Kentucky. She explained to him that the younger children would have greater educational opportunities. The situation that existed where we lived, would require me to room and board to go to high school 18 miles away in the town of Morehead. Usually children didn't finish the eighth grade and those that did, very seldom went to high school. This was most always due to financial reasons.

Father didn't think that high school was really necessary and you could help out on the farm as a regular worker. Finally, April 1942, dad rented a small farm in Pleasant View, WV, just across the highway from Guyan Valley High School. We moved there near the end of April. Our moving to this small community was a great cultural shock. Our farm in Kentucky was quite a distance from other farms and the general store was about eight miles away. We had to ride horseback to go to the store and I went very few times as my older siblings would go. I recall that we traded chickens and eggs for certain items in the store. Dad would also trade smoked hams to this store for groceries.

Now we lived in a small community with a store across the highway, with automobiles passing every so often, a Greyhound Bus passing morning and evening, and school busses parked across the road in front of the high school! There was a small restaurant with a Wurltzier Juke Box — what living? A Baptist Church, and four miles north and south were two other communities. What a shock this was, however it was so exciting to realize there was a world like this to experience. We had electric lights, a gas cookstove and running hot and cold water, and a bathtub. We had an ice box that the "ice man" filled up about every four days. I think it was about 1945 when we got a gas Servel Refrigerator. The toilet was located outside, some distance from the house!

My time in the Air Force, coming home and returning to college was certainly a turning

point in my life. Another was when I met my wife to be, Gloria Watson, in late1955 and marrying her in May 1956. She helped me very much by working at the Chesapeake Potomac Telephone Company while I attended college full time. My graduating from college is another. The birth of our children was a wonderful experiences in my life.

# Chapter 22

## HOBBIES?

At a very young age, I was permitted to hunt squirrels and rabbits. We had a dog on the farm that assisted in these activities, especially when we missed the rabbit when we fired, he would track the rabbit to an opening in the ground and we attempted to dig it out.

Prior to moving to West Virginia, I fished in ponds of water that had been formed by the creeks that passed on two sides of the farm where we lived. These fish were not very large, however mother always helped us clean them and she would fry them for us. When we lived in WV we fished in the Guyan River which was located some distance in back of the high school. My brother and I enjoyed this very much. We had friends that loaned us a boat and we would set trot lines across the river. This was a heavier line that we tied to the bank on each side of the river. The hooks were attached to smaller lines that were tied to the trot line. We would bait the hooks, holding the trot line across the front of the boat as we slowly moved across the river. We always had a fire on the river bank and about four hours later we would run the trot line and remove the fish from it.

I hunted squirrels when we lived in West Virginia. I built a cabin near the top of a hill, up the hollow on the farm we lived on. I had a small cooking stove, small table and a bunk bed in it. I would go there, stay all night and get up before daylight and go a few hundred feet and wait for the squirrels to start feeding. What an enjoyment it was to be in the outdoors.

I had a sign on the cabin door, "Hunters Welcome". I had information on the inside of the door asking any visitor to leave the cabin as they found it and to enjoy themselves while they used the cabin. When I left for the Air Force and was home on leave two years later, someone burned the cabin down. I want to think that they got the stove too hot and it set the logs on fire and caused this.

You may say that sports was a hobby during high school, however I made coaching a part of my profession. My first year coaching basketball was in 1958-59. I had completed my student teaching at Cammack Jr. High School in Huntington, WV with Hal Greer, a star of the Marshall College basketball team. Hal had been drafted by the Syracuse Nationals of the NBA. In April of 1960, I had our basketball banquet at the Coffee Shop Restaurant in Ironton, Ohio and Hal Greer served as the speaker. I will never forget when I called him about being our speaker, he said, Homer, I have difficulty speaking in front of an audience. I said Hal, put together some of the experiences you have had the past year as a rookie in the NBA. Hal related many experiences of his first year in the NBA and the audience loved his talk. Later the Syracuse Nationals became the Philadelphia 76'ers...

I enjoy working on my computer. I have became involved in genealogy and have researched some of my ancestors. The computer has helped me very much while I served as a grand officer for the Ohio Order of the Eastern Star. I utilized the e-mail very much as a Grand Trustee of the Order of the Eastern Star.

Our vacations have always been an important time for our family. When the children were younger, we enjoyed going to the beach, the Smoky Mountains, Museum of Natural History in Chicago and other trips. The boys have expressed in later years that they thought their best vacation was the time we camped in a tent in the Smokies and we fished for mountain trout in the stream high in the mountains! My wife Gloria says she faked what a good time she had on this vacation!

I am involved in the senior golf leagues at our golf course here where we live and I enjoy it very much. I do not take it too serious and I guess you could say it is an enjoyable hobby of mine.

# Chapter 23

## MARRIAGE

In the fall of 1955, I had returned from the Air Force and was living with my parents. I was working again for the C&O Railway. I was sitting on my mother's front porch and I noticed a car stop across the highway in front of the house and a young lady got out and went into the store. I yelled to mother and said I was going down to the store to get some bread and she said we have bread, we do not need any. I said I will get something from the store. I rushed to the store and saw this blond, wearing short shorts paying for a pack of cigarettes. I said to her, "you don't smoke those, do you?". She said, these are for my father in the car. This was my first time that I had seen Gloria. In later years, she told me that when she returned to the car, her mother asked her, did you meet that boy that came into the store? We know his parents and they are a nice family, what did you think of him? She said I think he is an "Ass".

I met her later on the next week and we began to date. The following spring, I married Gloria Ann Watson, May

4, 1956! Kyle Garretson, a high school classmate, was my best man. He was one of the boys that went with me to Detroit to work after high school graduation. The maid of honor was Sharon Pratt.

We lived at mom and dad's house for 26 days after we married. We moved to 1229 ½ Sixth Avenue, Huntington, West Virginia..We purchased food from a grocer near my mother's house, for the first four weeks we were in our apartment in Huntington. I have a list of the items we purchased on the original bills the grocer used to charge the items to us, these are in my scrap book!

I was continuing to go to college in the summer. Gloria had got a job at the Chesapeake and Potomac Telephone Company as a telephone operator and our apartment was about one block from the telephone offices. Gloria usually worked the second shift, getting off at 11:00 P.M. She made $42.50 per week and with my income on the G.I. Bill, we got along just fine. I did not take a job as I wanted to concentrate on my studies.

I usually picked her up in my '51 Ford Custom and we would go to Stewarts Drive Inn for hot dogs and root beer. This drive inn was started in 1932 and is still open today. This was a great and happy time, going to school, working, and visiting parents on the weekend. These hot dogs are sold at Marshall University football games today.

# Chapter 24

## PETS

When I lived on the farm in Kentucky, I always remember having dogs at our house. They were used primarily as watch dogs, however they helped us rabbit hunt.

When our twin sons were about 3 years old, we had a black and white dog that was their pet. It was very loyal to the family and was outstanding with neighbor children playing with our children. This dog passed away in 1964.

We built our new house in the summer of 1965 and Gloria's father said he had a German Shepard for the boys, if we would come to Chicago and get him. We went out to her parents for a few days and became familiar with the dog. When we were coming home, he got sick in the car and we had to stop a few times with him. He was a very faithful and playful dog for the family. He especially was a great watch dog. We had a neighbor tell us that another man who lived not too far from our house killed this dog. This dog had fathered a litter of pups and we kept one and raised it. He was very friendly and protective of the house. He got killed by a vehicle as he was trying to follow a truck that had a dog in the back of it. This was about one-half mile from the house and Tim and Jon, our twin sons took a shovel and buried him near the road where he got killed.

Our last dog was a Keeshond. Gloria, my wife, had a stroke in1989. We visited Todd, our youngest son in Zanesville, Ohio around Christmas time. Gloria and Todd and his wife were walking through the mall and went through a pet store. Gloria saw this small Keeshond and put her hand up next to the window and the puppy rubbed his head against the glass, trying to touch her hand. She liked the puppy and they told me about it when they came back to the house. They said it was $350.00. I said no one should pay that much for a dog! When we got home, Todd called his mother and asked her to ask me, if the dog was there next week could we get it. I said it will be sold before then, but that would be OK.

Todd called us to come to their house that coming week end. When we got there. he had the puppy in the recreation room with newspapers torn up all over the floor. Later on I was to find out that he purchased the puppy the day after we left. What a wonderful pet. Her name was Kisha. This breed of dog was brought to this country from Holland in 1926. She passed away in 2002 at the age of 13 and is buried in the back yard of our former house in Oak Hill.

# Chapter 25

## ACCOMPLISHMENTS I'M MOST PROUD OF

I am thankful that I had the opportunity to go to high school and participate in extra-curricular activities. I enjoyed athletics, especially basketball in which I was on three Sectional Championship teams and two Regional runner up teams. I still have one Sectional medal and two runner-up medals. I am most proud of learning to play the drums and participating in the high school band. I made All State Band for three years at our annual Band Festival in Huntington, West Virginia. I still have these medals and I was so proud of them when they were awarded to me by Mr. Louie Hoff, our band director.

I consider it an accomplishment to have left for work in an automobile plant in Detroit, Michigan, just two days after graduating from high school, and returning 90 days later to enroll in Marshall College. A great experience was being in the Marshall Marching and Concert Band the fall of 1951. Our son Tim, has a picture of me in the band uniform of Marshall College.

I went into the Air Force, thinking I would return and further my college education on the G.I. Bill. This is what I did. I was the only person to graduate from college in my family, that consisted of eleven, and I feel this is one of my highest accomplishments.

My marriage to a wonderful person is my greatest accomplishment. This is very hard to put into words. Gloria, my wife is such a great person. She is a wonderful mother and help mate. She returned to school and finished Rio Grande College after our youngest son was in kindergarten. The three wonderful sons are a combined accomplishment of Gloria and I.

I became a high school principal, after teaching and coaching for five years. The years I spent in school administration, is also one of my highest accomplishments. The work was very rewarding and the benefits at the time and during retirement have been very good.

I was appointed in the Grand Line of Officers for the Ohio Order of the Eastern Star in 1996, by Roberta David, Associate Grand Matron from Dayton, Ohio and Charles Hagley, the Associate Grand Patron of Ohio from Chilliocothe. In October I came out on the Cleveland Ohio Convention Center floor as the Grand Sentinel of the Order. The next two positions I was elected by the membership.

I was the Associate Grand Patron my second year and my third year, 1999, I was the Worthy Grand Patron for Ohio, serving with Peggy Wright, Worthy Grand Matron. This required many presentations, and especially much memory work. She had many inspections and visitations that we attended in Eastern Star Chapters throughout Ohio. Peggy and her husband Dave are from Frazeysburg,

Ohio. I traveled with the 18 Grand Officers throughout Ohio. We have our annul Grand Chapter Convention in the fall of the year.

I have completed five years as a Grand Trustee of the Grand Chapter of the Order of the OES of Ohio. I wish to thank Past Grand Matron, Roberta for giving me the wonderful opportunity to serve the Grand Chapter of Ohio, Order of the Eastern Star.

# Chapter 26

## FAMILY FEUDS

This story was told by my mother in our family for many years. She said that a favorite bread that she made for dad when she was first married was corn bread. This was made from corn meal, a small amount of flour, bacon grease and butter milk. She said the buttermilk made the best corn bread.

Buttermilk was made on the farm by putting milk, in which the cream had raised to the top, in a churn. The milk would be churned for about 30 minutes and the butterfat came to the top of the milk, leaving buttermilk on the bottom. The butterfat was worked down, putting the butter in butter molds that made a nice mold of butter.

Mom said she was getting buttermilk from Easter, her mother-in-law, for some time, then she stopped giving it to her. She told mom she didn't have any. Mother wondered why she quit giving her the buttermilk. She heard from a neighbor nearby that Easter was upset with her and Easter said she would rather pour the buttermilk

over the bank than give it to that "big headed Beulah."
Mother said this caused a strained relationship for many
years. I asked mother, why did she think that grandmother
called her "big headed"? Mother said that she kept a very
clean house, had put cardboard over the walls, papered
newspaper over the cardboard, then papered the walls
with a very inexpensive wallpaper. She said she made
curtains to put over the windows, which grandmother
didn't do. Mom said evidently grandmother thought she
was making her house so much more presentable than
hers that she resented it.

In 1940 my father asked an older brother to go to
the house of the two brothers who had been hired to
raise our tobacco base on the halves. This meant that they
would take care of the tobacco crop and would get half
of the money when it was taken to the tobacco auction.
The reason father asked my brother to go to their house
was to inform them that they would not be continuing
work on the tobacco crop unless they improved their
work habits, as the crop wasn't being properly attended
to. This occurred on a Sunday evening as dad had already
left for the 18 miles back to Morhead to catch a train to
his work in Huntington, WV.

My brother, Cartmal went to the house of these two
individuals. He later told me that he was lying on the
ground, with his head resting upon the side of a sled.
This sled had 4 wooden standards about 6 foot high in
the holes on each side of the sled. He said he had his
hands behind his head to sort of serve as a cushion against
the sled. When he told the brothers what dad said, one
jumped, grabbed a standard and started hitting him over
the head. He said the fact that he had his arms the way

they were probably kept him from getting killed. He said he saw stars, was almost knocked out but rolled over and got to his feet and said Walter, "if I catch you, I will end you". He said it was just at the edge of dark and Walter had a white shirt on and he began to chase him through the trees, catching him and gave him a severe beating and used his knife. He said he shouldn't have done this, however he was so mad, after almost being killed, that he wasn't thinking straight.

Walter's family finally got him to Morhead to the doctor and he lived. Needless to say these families were going to get Cartmal. Cartmal left on a train from Morhead and went to Antigo, Wisconsin to work on a dairy farm of some of dad's relatives. It was in Wisconsin, September 19, 1940 that Cartmal joined the Army and was sent to Camp Claiborne, Louisiana for training. He was originally a part of the 82$^{nd}$ Motorized Division. He became a member of the 101$^{st}$ Airborne Division on August 15, 1942.

I can not think of a family feud existing in our family. Gloria and I have always expressed our opinion, and we have recognized that we are sometimes wrong in an opinion and we are ready to accept others ideas and opinions.

# Chapter 27

## FAMOUS PEOPLE I'VE MET

In the fall of 1954, I attended a concert given by Nat King Cole at The Harolds Club in Reno, Nevada. After the concert he came off stage and many of us got to talk with him. I always thought he was one of our great performers.

In 1955 I was traveling by train from Reno, Nevada to home. The word got passed around that "Sugar Ray" Robinson was traveling on the train. Some of the people on the train had been back to the club car and were returning. They said that they had a chance to meet Sugar Ray. I had my Air Force uniform on and I went to the club car. Before long I was nearby and had the opportunity to meet Sugar Ray Robinson - the boxer. At the time, I felt this was a very "big deal".

I met Hal Greer when I was going to Marshall College. Hal played basketball for the college and was drafted by the National Basketball Association into the Syracuse Nationals. Hal's Syracuse Nationals became the Philadelphia Seventy Sixers. Hal was an outstanding individual as well as an outstanding basketball player. He was recognized in his hometown of Huntington, WV by the city naming a Boulevard after him.

I had the opportunity to met Hubert Humphrey, a senator running for nomination for president, when he was campaigning in Huntington, WV. This was in 1959, I think. In later years when I was serving as the high school principal and a delegate to the North Central Accrediting Association, I saw him at the Palmer House Hotel in Chicago, Illinois. He was a keynote speaker for our annual convention. I was serving on the examination committee for the state of Nebraska.

In the fall of 1965, I attended some seminars at Ohio University in Athens, Ohio. I had the privilege to meet Jesse Stewart, the author from Kentucky. I had read many of his books and enjoyed the discussions at the seminars, especially his experiences as a young teacher and high school principal in the mountains of Kentucky.

I think it was in the early 70's when I met "Bo" Shembechler, the football coach at Michigan. He was serving as the speaker for the Ironton Tribune Sports banquet that was held at South Point at the Holiday Inn. I recall how he began his talk. There were trophies lined up on the table in front of the speakers podium. Bo is introduced and he began, "men, see these trophies here?, five years from now, no - one year from now, you will not be able to buy a cup of coffee with a trophy you get here". He continued with an outstanding talk about how athletics could help you become an important individual to society and to your family and where you should place your values.

In the spring of 1976, I attended the Ohio High School State Track Meet in Columbus, at the Ohio State football stadium - "The Horseshoe". My sons were in the track meet. We were walking around the track prior to it getting started and Tim, one of my sons, saw Woody Hayes, the famous Ohio State football coach, sitting near by. A few people had been talking to him and we went over to where he was seated. I introduced myself and Tim. Tim had a program book and had Woody to autograph it. Tim has this booklet today.

In 1976, I was at a Sports Banquet for the Tri-State region at Marshall University. This was at the Holiday Inn, in South Point, Ohio. The speaker for this banquet was "Rocky" Blair a football player for the Pittsburgh Steelers. After the meeting we got to meet him. Athletics has always been an integral part of our family.

# Chapter 28

## HAVE I GROWN IN SPIRIT?

I was raised in a family that attended church regularly. I realized that a greater power than ourselves was important to believe in. As I got older, less emphasis was placed upon my spiritual well being. Mother felt that the military service had affected my outlook in this area.

I was always pursing my goals. I didn't think I had time to get involved in the spiritual realm, as I was so busy.

In the summer of 1965, we were having our new house built. As construction progressed, I had some disagreements with the subcontractors, one in which had left some work undone and I called the company and he had to return from Columbus, Ohio to finish the work that he had told them he had finished. During this time, it seemed that the workers wanted to do their work as quickly as possible, and I was concerned with the quality of their work just as well as the expediency.

I had been told by the workers that I would enjoy the man that came to do our cement work on the house. This was the basement, family room and the garage. When he arrived, a black man and two boys in an old pick up truck, containing their tools, he introduced himself and the boys, asked where he could order the concrete?. I told him and he said to me, are you a Christian? I said, well and he said, really, what I mean, have you met the "Man"? And he immediately said we have to go order the cement.

Later on that day, I came to the house and he was on his knees, smoothing the cement in the basement. He was singing a spiritual song and the notes seemed to be floating out of the windows of the basement. I asked the two younger boys if this man carried on like this all the time? One of the boys said, "Mr., he is the happiest man in the world! Happiest, I thought, is this happiness in a basement finishing cement on your knees. He came out in a little while and told me to come back about three o'clock tomorrow that he would be finished. He then said, Williams, when you have time, take the greatest book that was ever written and read about the greatest teacher that ever lived. He said I'll see you tomorrow.

The next day I came over to the house and they were finishing their work. He said I want to show you my work and he did. He said, "if you have any concerns, tell me. I did the best I could do with these hands, showing me his hands, that God gave me to work with". They finished their work and as the battered, old pickup truck pulled upon the road, he stopped, looked back and said, don't forget to read about The Greatest Teacher that ever lived.

I, being in education, began to wonder about this gentleman's words and how they related to a master teacher. This common laborer had reached me by the simplicity of his sharing his way of life in his daily work. He left a hatchet in the basement where he had been working. I feel this is a reminder of the way he did his work and his way of leaving a part of himself with me - a hatchet that I always use in some chores around the house.

In the fall of that year, I made a commitment and turned my life over to Christ. This was in a revival in the Evangelical United Breather Church in Oak Hill. Rev. Harold Sturm, our minister, baptized me in Lake Jackson, which is about a mile from our home in Oak Hill at the time..

I have since served our church in many lay positions as well as serving as president of the District Mens Organization. I also became a certified Lay Speaker and have spoke in many churches.

I have served as a member of Lay Witness Teams. These teams were made up of persons from adjoining states. I attended missions to Kentucky, West Virginia, Ohio, and Indiana. I have also served on the Administrative Board and the Pastor Parish Relations Committee of the Faith United Methodist Church in Oak Hill.

# Chapter 29

## PERSON'S WHO HAVE BEEN A SPECIAL INFLUENCE IN MY LIVE

I would be remiss if I didn't list my mother and father as being the two most influential people in my life. Mother would always show her love to us children through her caring attitude and her devotion to the family and to our father. She could be firm in her decisions to discipline and remain a loving mother. Mother took care of all the discipline, as father was away at work. When he came home, about every two weeks, he brought candy and was more interested in having fun with us.

Dad was a friend to us and he never utilized any harsh discipline. He was a father that always provided for the family. I never knew my father not to have a job. He worked away on the Chesapeake & Ohio Railway.

I recall dad telling about people years ago, saying there was no work for them, and he said he went to Lewis County, an adjoining county, and cut corn for five cents a shock. This was twenty four hills square to make one shock of corn. He said he would start cutting early before sun up and cut some evenings by the light of the moon. He said if he could cut fifty shocks a day he made $2.50. This was when my older brothers and sisters were young and I hadn't been born. Dad was always a provider for the family.

My oldest brother, George T. Williams always had a significant influence upon me. I recall his financial help to mom and dad when our house burned in 1936. He told about his experiences he had when he traveled throughout the country and the world. He had many interesting trips to other countries when he was in the Merchant Marines during World War II. His formal education consisted of finishing the eighth grade then going to Breckenridge Training School in Morhead, Ky. He then taught one term of school in the one room school that he had attended. Mother said after the one term of school that he taught, he said he could earn more money traveling about the country. Mother said he left and six months later she received a letter from him and he was serving as a guide in the Adirondack Mountains. This wandering he seemed to have about him, appealed to me as well as his interest in education. I think his becoming a teacher helped to influence me to want to become a teacher.

Some teachers I had were Louie Hoff our band director and Coach Richard Ware. Coach Ware was my basketball and baseball coach. Each one of them demonstrated and understanding of working with young people. I admired them for their dedication to their work.

Mr Walter Midkiff was my Typing teacher for two years in high school. He always dressed as a professional, shirt, tie, sport coat or suit. He always seemed to be so business oriented about his approach to teaching his subjects. He was well prepared and so understanding when dealing with his students. He was an educator that you could easily say, what a professional.

My wife Gloria, has been such a great influence on me. She has been an outstanding mother for our children and a positive person, with a gregarious personality that others feel so pleased and comfortable being in her presence. She returned to school after the children were born, finishing college in three and one half years. She then started teaching in the elementary school in Jackson, Ohio. I could never have had a better marriage partner than you Gloria! I love you.

Once and awhile there occurs an individual that you meet that has unbelievable characteristics of relating to others. A professor of Physical Education at Marshall College, Otto "Swede" Gullickson was that individual to me. He exhibited those abilities to cause you to challenge yourself to achieve your objectives and set higher goals. He did this in an atmosphere of pleasantness, firmness, joyousness, loudness, greatness and caring. I had him as an instructor as a freshman in college. He was a great teacher that I had the pleasure to receive instruction from at Marshall College.

Rev. Harold Sturm, was a minister of the church we attended after moving to Oak Hill. He illustrated what the field of pastoral ministries encompassed. He was a true friend and a loving minister of our church, The Evangelical United Bretheren. He was dedicated and worked such long hours and continued to have an enthusiasm and energy for his work.

# Chapter 30

## SPECIAL GIFTS I'VE RECEIVED

Mother made me two quilts and three quilt tops since we've been married. She gave me the quilts that she quilted herself. One was the Bow Tie quilt and the other one was the Log Cabin. My favorite quilt top was the last one she gave me in 1981, she was 88 years old. This one is the Postage Stamp quilt.

In April of 2006 I had the three quilt tops quilted. This was just prior to our leaving to live in South Carolina. When I went to the lady's house to pick up the quilts, she said, "do you realize what you have in one of these bags"? I said yes, the postage stamp quilt, it was so difficult and mother spent so much time making it. The lady said no, you have an heirloom. The quilt made out of different color and shaped pieces of silk is special, you see, she did special stitching around each piece, with many different designs in the stitches. This type of work, you very seldom see today".

A very special gift I have is a panorama picture of Lake Michigan in Chicago. Mother, Dad, Kenneth, my 1 ½ year older brother were attending the Worlds Exposition in 1933. It shows the name of the exhibitors at this exhibition and their locations along the lake front. When our house burned in 1936, my sister pulled one item out of the house, a chest of drawers which included this picture which was rolled up in a paper tube. My mother give this to me in 1981.

I was given an old German Army field radio case (hard plastic like case) from WWII. My brother Cartmal, who was in the 101st Airborne was in Europe when he got this radio case. This was one of the items he brought home after the war.

My mother gave me an old upholstered arm chair. The chair had been given to her by my oldest brother George who was working in Cincinnati, Ohio at the time. His landlady give him the chair as he had told her about our house burning and we lost everything. This was after the house burned and we just had got into our new house that dad had built. The chair was shipped by train to Morhead, Ky and an older brother went to Morhead and brought the chair on top of his car to our house on North Fork of Tripplett creek. I found on the underneath side of the chair, writing, stating, Upholstered by Henry Shufotall, March 8, 1923, Cinn. O. I gave the chair to Charlie Howard, a janitor in our school system, in the spring of 2006, knowing that I would not move it to our new house in South Carolina.

A gift that Gloria, my wife, received from her Grandmother Linnie Ramey, who raised her father, was an old Martha Washington platter. You could tell that it had been used very much. Linnie said she put it in the warmer on the kitchen wood cook stove many, many times with food on it. Linnie also give us a round kitchen table. It has a leaf that can be inserted in the table. This table was made around 1910 from hard maple wood. We have it today in the nook of the family room in the lower level of our house.

The items just mentioned have a great sentimental value. A part of our family's heritage seems to be encased in these items.

# Chapter 31

## MY LIFE TODAY

I retired from the Oak Hill School System in Oak Hill, Ohio with thirty eight years of service. With my Air Force time, I had almost forty two years.Gloria retired from the Jackson City School System.

We were active in our church, the Faith United Methodist Church, formerly The Evangelical United Brethern of Oak Hill. Gloria and I served on the Administrative Board and she was in the Women's Society of the church. I served on the pastor Parish Relations Committee and was Chairman in 2005-2006.

In May 2006 we sold our house in Oak Hill and bought a house in a Dell Webb active lifestyle community in Indian Land, South Carolina.

We enjoy visiting our children and the grandchildren. We have eight grandchildren, 7 girls and one boy. Our son, John lives in Iowa. His oldest daughter completed college in 2006. She took training in Australia and served as a missionary in Africa. She was sponsored by a Lutheran church in DeMoines, Iowa. She has two sisters, Kay Lynn and Jena Lee. They are both going to college. Our son Tim, has four children. The oldest, John is a sophomore in college and is on the golf team. Jane will be going to Ohio State University in the fall of 2008. Sarah and Margaret are in high school. Our youngest son Todd, has one daughter, Camryn. His wife couldn't have children and Camryn came along after 17 years of marriage. What a joy Camryn is. She is seven years old.

I spend quite a bit of time on my computer. I joined Ancestry.com and do quite a bit of research of my family's history. I also utilize the computer to download pictures from my digital camera to send to our children and grandchildren. The children send pictures to us as well as video cams of the children.

I have been golfing for about seven years. Our oldest son, Tim belongs to a country club in Painesville, Ohio. I visit there and go golfing with him and John, our grandson. I joined a seniors golf league when I lived in Oak Hill and now I am member of a seniors league here at Sun City Carolina Lakes in South Carolina..

In January and February of 2004 and December, January & February of 2005,my wife and I stayed at Myrtle Beach, SC. The winters were mild and I played quite a bit of golf with three other men, two of them were from the town of Proctorville, Ohio.

Our boys and their families visited us in Myrtle Beach during the Christmas holidays of 2004. Tim and his family came from Chardon, Ohio, his twin brother John came from DeMoines, IA., and Todd and his family came from Charlotte, NC. We had a three bedroom condo and I rented a one bedroom condo while they were there. We all had a great time.

Our son's and their families came to our new house here in South Carolina during Christmas 2006. We moved into the new house October 2, 2006. This is an active lifestyle community. It has a large activities building with many activities, such as water aerobics, physical fitness room, computer room, card playing area, billiard tables, art room, woodworking room, craft room, industrialized kitchen, walking track at the second level and others. The bocce ball courts, tennis courts, outside pool and golf course are other activities. There are walking trails throughout the community. Plans for the near future is to have a supermarket, drug store, medical building, CVS, bank, and fast food enterprise in this community. Gloria will be able to ride our golf cart and take care of the grocery shopping!! We feel we have been blessed. We have a good retirement and our children have good wives and the grandchildren are great. God has really blessed our home.

# Chapter 32

## LESSONS I'VE LEARNED

I think one of the greatest lessons of life I've learned came from my mother. I was always told that I was an important individual, however I was to never think that I was better than another person. I was taught to never give up on myself or what I wished to acompolish. I was told that if you feel you have "fallen down", don't lay there, get up and continue to do you best, and your best will always do.

These teachings from mother helped me to become confident and self assured. I tried to instill this attitude in our children. One boy became a pharmacist, and is married to pharmacist. His twin brother became a teacher and coach, went into insurance then back into coaching and is married to a nurse. The youngest son is in hospital finance and is married to a pharmacist.

I've learned that it is important to have goals in life and to acompolish set objectives to reach those goals. The image I have of myself has always been that I can acompolish that task, an usually I always did.

I've learned that positive thinking is important. A person that is positive is someone that others enjoy being around. The world we live in seems to portray many negative images and it is important not to get caught up in this type of thinking. I always felt that I could find good in an individual and it is important to encourage the things that are positive about a person.

I think the environment that I was raised in at home taught me so many positives that it wasn't that much of a challenge for me to accomplish many goals in my life. My father was such a hard worker, whether it was his job on the railroad or the work that he was always doing when he came home to the farm on the week ends. I think from being around him, taught me the importance of a good work ethic.

A great lesson that I've learned is the importance of having a religion that gives me a foundation for a belief in the hereafter. I believe that I have a Creator that will help sustain and support me throughout life and provides me a dwelling place for eternity.

My attitude toward death is one that has been developed from early childhood. I believe there is a place that has been prepared for all of us, after death, who have lived a life that has been pleasing to our God. The Bible tell us that this place is called heaven and we should not worry too much when a person dies and has prepared themself for this dwelling place

# Chapter 33

## A BIG BLIZZARD

In the spring of 1970, during Easter break, we were going to Melrose Park, near Chicago, where Gloria's parents lived. Our twin boys were eleven years old and Gloria's sister, Canzaza's two children, Debbie and Eric were with us. We were traveling in a 1968 Delmont Oldsmobile. We were near Valpraso, Indiana, on Route 35 and there was about six inches of snow along side of the road. We continued some distance and the road became more hazardous. We passed a Holiday Inn and noticed the parking lot was full of cars. We continued for about two miles and the snow was very wet and packed down on the four lane road creating hole like structures in the deeply packed down snow. All traffic was stopped in front of us, only one lane available for the cars to move. Once and awhile we would see a few cars go by on the other side of the road and we would move about 50 foot at times and wait for thirty to fifty minutes before we could go on again.

I got out of the car with an old Army blanket wrapped around me, I have this blanket today, and went to the car in front of me and talked to the man inside. Eric was scared that Uncle Homer would get hurt outside the car! We decided that there was very little traffic coming from the other direction and if he followed me, we would cross over the median and travel in the wrong direction until we saw car lights coming and we would cross back over to our lane of traffic. We did this about four times and when we crossed back over, a semi tractor trailer truck was stopped coming our way and he said it was impossible to go any further as cars couldn't get through the packed down snow. We were at an intersection in which a road came from our right. A small car with two college students stopped and asked about our roads from where we came from. We told him we were going to Melrose Park and it was very bad where we had come from. He said it was clear where he came from. He gave us directions, go about four miles North, then West and the road is practically clear all the way.

We arrived about seven hours late and we saw on TV the next day pictures that were taken by a news helicopter in which people had to abandon their cars and were taken in by people in farm houses. How lucky we were that we didn't try to go beyond where the trucker told us the snow was so deep that we could not travel.

# Chapter 34

## TRIPS AND VACATIONS

In 1938, mother took my brother, Kenneth and I on a train to Antigo, Wisconsin. She had passes for our travel that were furnished by The C & O Railway Company for employees. We were going to visit the Bill Brown family who was related to my father. They owned a large dairy farm and mother had told us about the level laying land and how beautiful it was with large clear running streams on the land.

Mother had prepared fried chicken, cookies and other food for us to eat when we were on the train. Kenneth and I had never experienced this type of travel before. Kenneth and I were in one seat and mother was in a seat across the isle from us. She got the food out and gave to us and we began to eat. I noticed Kenneth holding his head over and acting as if he was trying to hide his face when he took a bite of food. You must remember, this was the first time we had ever been on a train eating food in front of strangers, so our social skills seemed to be lacking. I didn't let any of it bother me and I talked, eat and enjoyed the meal. A man in the seat behind us gave a banana to Kenneth and I.

We arrived in Antigo, WI and on to our destination at the Brown family farm. I never had seen a dairy farm and was appalled at how large it was. The many cows, lining up in rows in the barn for milking. There was a large bull with a ring in his nose and a large chain attached to the ring. Mr. Brown said he was a very mean animal and he had to control his behavior in that manner. I recall one evening when mother was talking in the living room, Kenneth and I climbed upon the cabinet in the kitchen and obtained a couple of Graham crackers and they were so good.

In 1940 mother took the children by train to Cincinnati, Ohio to visit with a son and two daughters. My older brother, George lived in a rooming house and my sisters Ida Mae and Lorena lived in a house nearby. This was my first visit to a large city. My brother, Kenneth and I slept on the floor in the living room and we could hear the street cars at night. When we heard one coming, we would jump up, go to the window and watch the car passing, and as it went under certain wires, the trolley cables made large balls of sparks and we thought this was so thrilling to see.

Our older sisters told us they were taking Kenneth and I to Coney Island Amusement Park the next day. They said we would go by boat, The Island Queen, docked downtown Cincinnati and we would take it to Coney Island. We were instructed never to leave too far from them, that the crowds were large and they didn't want us to get lost. Just before we docked, Kenneth wasn't with us and my sisters got quite hysterical. Ida notified the Captain and they called out Kenneth's name not to get off the boat but remain on the boat nearby where passengers were getting off. We waited until everyone had got off the boat, and – no Kenneth. Ida and Lorena said we will get off and go into the park and see if we can find him. We sat down, not far from where there was a ride that consisted of small planes that went around and around. They asked me if I wanted to ride and I said I would and when the ride stopped, here came Kenneth running down the steps coming from the ride. What a lecture he received and he never got far from my sisters again.

In the summer of 1961, I went to Melrose park with Gloria and the twin boys. We stayed with Gloria's parents and I worked at a service station. We went to a lake in Wisconsin where her father had a small trailer and a boat docked. We did some fishing and this was enjoyable, especially for the children. I recall one Saturday, we all went to fish for the week end and the weather was somewhat overcast, but no severe storms were predicted. We gassed up the boat. Tim, John and their grandfather and I left the shoreline to go a great distance out into the lake to fish. A sudden storm came up, a ferocious wind, heavy rain with the waves increasing in height. Dad Watson said to head straight for the nearest shore, in a straight line as fast as possible. We arrived at the shoreline just in time. The wind had increased and was blowing at a very high speed. We pulled the boat up on the shore, run some distance and into an old shack with an old army cot in it. We stayed there until the storm subsided and went back across the lake. There were boats turned over and things were torn up on the shore. We were lucky.

When I applied for work at the service station, in Melrose Park, I was interviewed by the owner. During the interview, the owner called to the manager to come into his office. He said I want you to meet an honest individual. He introduced me to the manager and said "Homer says he wants to work for ninety days then return to Ohio to continue teaching and coaching". You know everyone who interviews for work says they want to work for a long time in our service station and after one or two paydays, that is the last of them. After the interview, the owner told the manager to work out my schedule.

The manager asked me to work for one week during the first shift and after that I would be on the third shift, from 11:00 PM to 7:00 AM. He said, "I get the feeling you are not too familiar with the life in the city". He asked what did the owner tell you about dropping money into the vault, which was wired to an alarm at the police station. I told him that the he said to drop money into the vault when it builds up to about $100.00, which may occur in about two to three hours. The manager said I wish to give you some advice, keep the money in the cash register until about 6:00 AM and make the drop, because if someone comes in to rob you, and you haven't made a drop, you have more money to hand over and they are less likely to hit you over the head so hard. I took this advise.

I must relate a couple of incidents that happened in the early AM on my shift. I was the only one at the station on the third shift. One night, after midnight, a car drove up to one of the pumps and I go to the car and ask how much gas, and he gets $1.25 worth, pays me and leaves. About forty five minutes later, a car drives up and asks for 75 cents worth of gas. I thought he looked like the man that had got gas earlier. About an hour and thirty minutes later, a car drives up and orders $1.00's worth of gas. I was looking nervously at the man and he said I see you are quite concerned. He said, "you see I get cars that have been repossessed." The people aren't making their payments and it is too dangerous to pick the cars up in their presence, so I work for a company and pick them up at night where there isn't a hassle. He said he had a helper that let him out nearby so he could go to the car and utilize the proper key. He showed me a large ring of keys that he was using.

One night about 3:00 AM, a black sedan pulled up to front door of the station, not at the pumps. I was very nervous as I could see 180 degree in front of the station and knew where I could push an alarm for the police to get there in ninety seconds. I went to the door and a man was sitting on the passenger's side with a sawed off shotgun between his legs. He said, "don't get alarmed, we're plain clothes detectives", and I wanted to ask you a question. He asked if any suspicious cars had come into the station to get gas in a hurry in the last thirty minutes or if I had seen any suspicious activity in the area in the last thirty minutes? I told him I hadn't seen anything. He said about thirty minutes ago, about five blocks from here, a maffia individual was entering the front of his house and was mowed down by automatic fire from an automobile. I continued my shift and went home the next morning quite nervous.

I had to work six days a week, however, Gloria and I found time to take the boys downtown to the Museum of Science and Industry and visited places of educational interest. This was so exiting for all of us.

In the summer of 1966, Gloria, the boys and I went to Burr Oak State Park near Athens, Ohio for a week end. We were staying in a cabin that wasn't very far from the lodge. When we got there, I told her that I had to return that night to give a response lecture on my Entered Apprentice Degree, as I was going into the Masons. I drove back to Oak Hill for the meeting and was quite late getting back to Burr Oak. Gloria was very upset as she couldn't get a fire started in the fireplace and it was very chilly. The next day we went fishing with the boys and had a good time fixing food at the cabin.

In the summer of 1967 we took a vacation to the Great Smoky Mountains. I had a 1961, four door Impala Chevrolet. I borrowed the carrier for the top of the car from Edgil Boggs and the tent that we would be camping in, from my brother Kenneth who lived in Huntington, WV.

We got to the Smoky Mountain National Park and checked on camp sites. They sent us to a camping area of the park and there was one site left. I don't recall the name of the campsite, however it wasn't too far from an old wooden building that was like an old hotel. Not too far up the hill from our campsite was an outdoor area that the Park Rangers gave educational presentations. Church was also held there on Sundays.

We traveled to Cades Cove. This contained the early settlement period and you took you car to tour the area. We had a map to guide us on our tour, showing points of interest as we stopped at the scheduled areas. One main stop was the Old Grist Mill, still in operation. We bought some corn meal that had been ground at the mill. We also saw a deer while traveling on this tour!

The boys said the most interesting part of this vacation was fishing for mountain trout, high up in the mountain streams. We caught the trout on dough balls. It was easy. I cleaned the fish and we fried them in our charcoal grill near by and years passed by before Gloria said she didn't like to camp, however, at the time she let on like she loved it!

In the summer of 1969, we went to Williamsburg, VA., and visited Monticello, the home of Thomas Jefferson. The motel we stayed in, had a small swimming pool and this sure was relaxing after walking so much during the hot day. The places of interest in Williamsburg were so educational and the visit to the home was very interesting. We took pictures of many places and one in particular was when the boys put their hands and head through a board that looked as if they were permanently shackled.

In the summer of 1970 we took a trip to Mammoth Cave State Park in Kentucky. Gloria's father had passed away and we took her mother and our children just to be together on a trip. We stayed in a motel and it had a pool and the boys had a tremendous time. Mom Watson sure seemed to enjoy herself being with the grand children.

One day we went to the cave entrance to take one of the tours. Gloria said she was afraid that she would get a cold and she waited for us outside with our youngest son. It was a walking tour and everything was going OK until our guide told us to look up. It was very high and stairs led up at a very steep angle and the walkway around the top of this room was protected by a protective railing.

Mom Watson said she wasn't used to heights and I said you walk one boy in front of you and I will walk one and we will move slowly with the group but do not look down. What a harrowing experience this was.

In the summer of 1971 we decided to take the family for their first beach vacation to Myrtle Beach, SC. I had talked to Bob Canter and he told me that "The Poindexter Motel" was a good place to stay, which is right on the beachfront. We stayed there for a week and I think it was one of the greatest vacations that our children ever experienced, as it was the first time to the beach, and everything was so exciting. I was in the ocean with our twin sons and they swam constantly, usually riding on a surf float. They ended up getting some skin removed from their chest from it the rubbing on the float. This was very painful, however, Gloria doctored and patched, and things continued to run smoothly! On our way home, we would stop by a roadside park and use our little two burner stove to cook hamburgers. This was living!

In 1972 we were going to visit Gloria's mother in Hollywood, Florida. On our way down, we went to Natchez, Mississippi. My youngest sister, Joyce and her husband lived there and we stopped for a couple of days. We went to the beach one day and Mark, my sisters boy and our boys had a great time. My brother in law, Paul had been transferred there as a Sears store manager.

We went on to Florida to grandmother Watson's house. She lived in a housing complex that had a swimming pool. We all liked going to the pool, however Gloria loves the beach and wanted to go there more, but her mother didn't like the sand and spent more time in the pool. The boys really liked this vacation, however I didn't get an air conditioner in the car and it was very hot traveling.

In the summer of 1974 we went to Biloxi, MI and New Orleans, LA. The water in the Gulf at Biloxi was quite different from that at Myrtle Beach. After our stay here, we went to New Orleans. What a city? Whiskey, women, and song seemed to be at our every turn, but what a historic city to visit. We took in so many of the sights of this historic city.

I will list a few of the other trips we took. In 1981, we took a trip out West. We stopped at the Petrified Forrest in Arizona and on to Flagstaff for the night. The next morning, very early, we went to the Grand Canyon. What a breathtaking experience as we entered and stopped at our first look out. We were speechless. From the Grand Canyon, we went south to Phoenix for a week. I had a meeting of the American Association of School Administrators. From here, we went to Bellflower, CA and visited my oldest brother, George and his wife. We also visited with a friend, Ercil Midkiff and his wife, who I went to high school with. After we returned home, we said this was one of our best solo vacations.

In 1991, Darrell and Martha Detty, friends of our's in Oak Hill since 1958, decided that we should go on a ocean cruise. Darrell and I told Gloria to arrange a three day cruise with the AAA office as we didn't know how we would like it. She did this and told us that she booked a seven day cruse on the Carnival Cruse ship, Celebration, to the Eastern Carribean. This was December 29, 1991. We celebrated on the dance floor as the New Year come in on the ship. We had a wonderful time.

In 1997, my wife, Gloria, who was President of District 24 Association of Order of the Eastern Star, organized a bus trip to Toronto, Canada. We saw the performance of "The Phantom of the Opera", which was outstanding. We had an evening dinner atop the tallest building, that contained a restaurant that slowly revolved 360 degrees. On our way back, we stopped at Niagra Falls for the day. The Maid of the Mist and the Cable Tram were two exciting events.

In the summer of 1999 we flew to Vancouver, boarded a ship, and went to Skagway, Alaska. We stayed overnight there and the next day took The White Pass Railway, a narrow gauge railroad for a great distance inland. We stayed overnight and the next day went up the Yukon River for quite a distance and then boarded large busses to Fairbanks, Alaska. We were with a group of Eastern Star members from Ohio. Friends from Oak Hill, Darell and Martha Detty, Rodney and Judy McCorkle and Judy's sister and brother in law were with us.

We rode the McKinley Explorer train from Fairbanks to Denali Park and stayed there overnight. We took busses into the park and the end of the trip got out of the buses and had hot chocolate from a large thermos container. We were told that bears loved chocolate and if the wind was blowing in the right direction, we may see a bear or two come our way. Just a few minutes later, the drivers said look, up on a small hill at the underbrush, came two bears. We got back into the busses and observed the bears up close. They finally walked away across a swamp like meadow. We went back to our cabin, ordered pizza and rested. The next day we took the train to Anchorage and flew from Anchorage to Seattle, Chicago and home.

In the summer of 2000, we went to Hawaii. We flew to the islands and took a cruse ship around the Islands. There were many places of interest that we visited, however the most daunting was the USS Arizona Memorial. We took a small boat out to the memorial and we saw the names of all who were entombed in the USS Arizona. You could see the film of oil still rising to the surface of the water, coming from the ship that was below us since 1941. Listening to a survivor of Pearl Harbor speak after touring the memorial was some experience. I had him sign a small newspaper of that period in time and I gave it to John, my grandson.

# Chapter 35

## A HAZARDOUS HUNTING TRIP

In November 1957 I decided to go rabbit hunting at my brother-in-laws house in Pt. Pleasant, WV. Scott Sage, my oldest sister's husband, said if I came up to his house, he knew where we could hunt. I checked with Kenneth, my older brother, and Gloria's younger brother, who was just out of high school and John Beckelheimer, the husband of an aunt of Gloria's. John said he would bring his beagle dog for the hunt.

It was Thanksgiving day, Gloria had to work at the telephone company, and my brother and I got in my car. John Watson and John Beckelheimer, with the dog, got in his pick up and we traveled to Point Pleasant. We stopped at Scott's house and my sister said she would try to have some lunch when we returned with the rabbit's.

Scott got in my car and directed us to travel about five miles out of Point Pleasant. We stopped near some large fields and rolling hills. Some of the area had grasses growing, corn stalks laying on the fields, sage brush growing on the higher rolling hills, with pine trees and other trees interspersed throughout the area. We began to circle the area, going quite a distance and jumped a few rabbits. The dog did and excellent job tracking the rabbits.

Some of the adjoining land had posted signs on it, NO HUNTING! John Beckelheimer had something for us to drink to try to stay warm. We traveled mostly on the un-posted land to hunt on, however the other land looked as if it may serve as a good place to hunt. We began to travel near a fence line on this land, however my brother stayed on the other side of the fence as we moved along hunting. All of a sudden, we saw a Jeep come traveling very fast through the field toward us. When he got there, it was a farmer and he asked us our names and said we were hunting on his property. My brother asked him if he was on his property and he said no, and my brother said you don't need to take my name. The farmer thanked us and left. We hunted for about another hour and started going to the road where we left our automobiles.

When we got to our automobiles, a Game Warden was there. He asked us if we had a good day hunting and we told him we did. He said that sure is a pretty beagle, does he do a good job tracking rabbits? John said he is my best beagle. A game warden had been killed about three weeks before, about fifty miles away. He had rushed upon some hunters and created quite a bit of excitement. This game warden said you guys are probably not who I'm looking for but I need to see your hunting license and check the names I have. He checked our license and said we had to follow him into town to the Justice of the Peace's Office. We got there and were told by the JOP that each of us had to pay a $23.00 fine. I had no money and I was on Thanksgiving break from college and I said, " well, I can't pay my fine and what then."? The Justice of the Peace said young man you can lay it out a few days in jail and the turkey you eat there will not be as good as what you would get at home. We sat there for awhile and Scott said "I'll have to run over to the house to get some money." We didn't know it but John Beckelheimer, who worked for the railroad had just got paid a few days before and had money. He said he would pay the fines and we could pay him back. I had a 20 gauge, single shot shotgun and asked him if he would take it for the twenty three dollars and he said he would. Needles to say, when I got back to Huntington quite late, Gloria was "so, so" upset and we were late leaving to go out to her mothers house and to my mothers house. This hunting trip was the talk of all family's involved for many years.

# Chapter 36

## LEARNING TO RIDE A BICYCLE, DRIVE A CAR AND USE A COMPUTER

In the fall of 1944, my older brother bought and old bicycle. He worked on it until he got in running condition and we began to learn to ride it. We would practice on the long driveway, from the road passing the front of our house to the barn some distance away. He would get me started, telling me to learn to coast and balance the bike as far as I could. I wrecked many, many times but learning to ride was an exciting adventure. We would practice until after it began to get dark and mother would call us to the house. My shirt would be completely wet from sweating. Finally I learned to ride and we went across the highway, in back of the high school to the baseball diamond and really enjoyed this newly learned skill.

In the spring of 1950, I wanted to learn to drive. Loren, an older brother who lived in Hurricane, WV would come over to our house on the weekend and let me drive his 1939 four door, stick shift Chevrolet. He always went with me and gave me instructions about safety and controlling the automobile. He said that when a person runs the car off the road that many severe accidents occur by the driver quickly turning the car back onto the road. He told me that when you run off the pavement, let off of the accelerator, slowly brake, and get the car back onto the highway. Once I was driving along and he said, "Homer run off the pavement and get it back on the road properly". I was quite nervous, however I did what he had instructed me to do to get the car back onto the highway properly.

At the end of the summer I was ready to take my drivers test. I had to go to Hamlin, WV as this was the county seat where the tests were given. Edgar Jennings (EJ) Midkiff, a friend who had just graduated from high school with my brother Kenneth, said he would take me over to get my test and I could use the car he was using. It was a 1949 Chevrolet that belonged to his grandfather, Lando Midkiff. This sure was a big favor for Lando to let me drive his car. I received my drivers license, dated August 8, 1950 - Sep 1, 1954. I have this license in a scrap book with the sale slips, pictures and other information of all the cars that I've ever owned, in chronological order. I bought my first car, a 1951 Ford in August 1955.

One of the most challenging tasks that I've tried to master, is learning to use the computer.I never had a lesson on the computer, however I became familiar with one in 1982 at the high school when I was high school principal. In 1985, as supervisor, I had a computer in my office, and used it quite a bit as in service education supervisor, cafeteria supervisor, curriculum supervisor, and special placement director.

Before I retired from teaching in 1996, I had a computer at home and it was very helpful in my work. After retiring, I purchased an updated system and became more familiar with using it. I used it very much for correspondence and making programs for meetings in the Eastern Star. As a Trustee of the Ohio Eastern Star, Grand Chapter of Ohio for five years, it certainly came in handy..

I utilize e-mail very much, have a scanner, a video-cam, and a digital camera in which I take pictures and e-mail to our children and grandchildren. They also send pictures to Gloria an I.

We have a web page here at the retirement community and Gloria and I have e-mail addresses in which we stay well informed about all of the activities that are scheduled daily.

# Chapter 37

## DESTINY RELATES THE BLACK TO ME

I gave much thought about this chapter as to whether it would fit into the story of my life. I know that it is only right that it be included.

When I was about six years old, mother read a book to all the children at home that was written by Harriet Beecher Stowe, "Uncle Tom's Cabin". I didn't realize that people were mistreated like the book explained and that they were black. Mother explained the prejudices toward the black people by many white people and the strife they encountered.

When we moved to WV, in 1942, my father took me to visit the "camp cars" where he worked. He was a cook and he said I want you to meet Blake, he is my black cook helper. This was the first time I had ever meet a black person. About a year later, dad and I were at the Huntington, WV train station and a train from Washington to Cincinnati stopped and a black conductor got off and my father said, "hello Blake, gave him a hug and said, I wondered where your next job took you". I noticed many people looked very curious at my father.

In 1947 I was a participant in the West Virginia annual band festival. There was a restaurant at the corner of 9th Street and 5th Avenue in Huntington, WV. There was a sign in the window that said, "No Colored Allowed". This was very hard for me to understand. I asked the question, why weren't they allowed? This restaurant, "The White Pantry" was in the national news later on.

I went to the Air Force in 1952, met blacks in basic training, went to supply school with them, worked with them and always got along. When I came from Alaska to Reno in 1954, we had a squadron basketball team and a black man named Mac worked in our supply unit on the flight line. The squadron basketball team participated against other teams on the air base. We had to play our games in a Catholic gym and I found out later it was because we had a black playing for us. I guess I had a lot to learn about people.

I kept asking Mac to come with me and we would go to Harold's club and eat, as the food was very good and quite cheap. He kept refusing me and I wouldn't give up on asking him. Later on, he said, Homer, will you go with me to eat where I eat after our next game? I said yes. After our next game, he took me ta dimly lighted area of town and we went into a dimly lit bar. We sat at the bar and ordered two beers. I could feel the atmosphere in the bar and seemingly many eyes were on us. We drank our beer and the bartender said, do you want another one, I said, no thanks this is enough. After leaving the bar, Mac said," Homer did you feel comfortable in our surroundings"? I said, no I was ill at ease. Mac said, wherever I go in your area of town, I always feel that way, and that is usually all the time. What a lesson he taught me.

When getting ready to do my student teaching, while in Marshall College, the director of student teaching called me into his office one day. He said you and Hal Greer will be doing student teaching together at Camack Jr. Hi. School. This was a very elite school at that time, having a picture of Rick Nelson in the trophy case as he had visited there. The director asked me to show up with Hal and go into the school together. I suppose he was concerned as to how Hal would be received. We showed up and there were many students applauding when we crossed the lawn to the school. Hal was a black basketball star for Marshall. He was drafted by the Syracuse Nationals and I had him to speak at my basketball banquet in 1960. I had four blacks that started for my basketball team that year.

I guess a most unusual happening occurred when I was building my house in 1965. The building contractor kept telling me that I would enjoy the cement contractor that would be working a few days later on. I met the "cement man", a black man with two young boys, one day as they arrived to the building site. He was in an old battered pick up truck, got out introduced himself and the boys. He said, Mr. Williams are you a Christian? I said, well, well, I and he said do you know the man?. Where can I order the cement, give me the directions. Later on that day, I came to where the house was being built and there was a spiritual song coming out the basement windows.

I looked through the windows, and working the cement on his knees, I turned and asked one of the boys, does that man carry on like that all the time? He said to me, "man he is the happiest man in the world".

When the days work was done the cement man, said to me, don't be in a hurry, but take time to read about the greatest teacher that ever lived, and what a life he had. I'll be finishing the job tomorrow about 3:00 PM and you be here.

The next day I arrived and he was finishing up. He said I want to show you my work and I hope you are pleased with it. I did the best I could do with the hands that God gave me to work with and I hope you and the wife will be happy in this house, but you will have to work hard to make it a happy home. The boys placed the tools in the truck and as he was driving away from the lot, he stopped the truck just before getting on the road, looked out the window, turning his head toward me, and said, remember what I said about the greatest teacher that ever lived, and drove away. I went home and told my wife all about this.

That fall our church was having a revival and I accepted Christ as my savior. I believe "HE" sent the "Cement man" my way.

My twin boys were very close to Joe Abbott who was black and attended our school. Joe's younger brother, James, was a close friend of our son Chris. He came to our house many times and Chris stayed at his house a lot. They were on the basketball team together. What a great family. James was killed in a car wreck in the eighth grade.

In the spring of 2000, a friend of mine told me about having two hip replacements. I told him I needed a hip replaced and would he recommend his doctor to me. He said, I sure would, he is one of the best, a black doctor in Columbus. I contacted his office, made arrangements for the operation and I got along just great. I am doing fine with all movements. You wouldn't know that I had a hip replaced.

I could say that destiny had a way for me to become acquainted with black people. My relationships with them and the manner in which they have always treated me has been outstanding.

I hope this chapter wasn't boring for you.

## The End

# MY LIFE CHRONOLOGY

1932    Birth, December 25

1933    Early spring, left at home with oldest sister to wean me as mother, dad, and Kenneth went to Worlds Exposition in Chicago

1936    House burned in early December, everything lost

1937    Train trip with mother and Kenneth to Antigo, WI

1939    Enters first grade at Hardeman one room school.

1941    Train trip with mother and Kenneth to Cincinnati, OH

1942    Left the security of the farm and moved away to WV in April

1947    Completed eighth grade at West Hamlin and entered high school in the fall

1948    First job to receive pay - Daily & Daily Telephone Line Construction, during the summer

1951    Graduated from Guyan Valley HS, worked summer Detroit, entered Marshall College

1952    Got a job with C & O Railway. Enlisted in the Air Force

1953    Left for Cheyene ,WY, then to Alaska at an Early Radar Warning Outpost, at Galena

1954    Stead Air Force Base, Reno, NV; Air Rescue Squadron

1955    Discharged from Air Force, bought my first car, 51 Ford, started back to work at C & O

1956    Returned to Marshall College on the GI Bill. Got married to Gloria Watson

1958    April: first new car - Ford Fairlane 500, September: first teaching job, twin sons born

1960    Obtained job teaching and coaching at Oak Hill High School

1961    Received Masters degree in January, worked during summer at Melrose Park, IL

1962    Attended Molecular Biology Institute during the summer, Ball State Teachers College

1963    In May our third son was born. Got the Oak Hill High School principals job in July

1965    Built a new house in Oak Hill, Started April 25 and we were in it by August 20th

1966    Joined the Masonic Order in Oak Hill

1968    Bought our second new car, Olds 88 Delmont. Wife starts Rio Grande College

1971    Elected president Oak Hill Chamber of Commerce. Gloria graduates from college

1972    Joined the Order of the Eastern Star. First vacation to Myrtle Beach

1977    Tim & John graduate from high school ands enter college

1981    Christopher Todd graduates from high school and enters college

1985   I finish twenty two years as high school principal and take supervisors job

1986   Thirtieth wedding anniversary, many family and others present

1989   My wife, Gloria, had a stroke

1991   Took a cruise with Gloria, Darell & Martha Detty to San Juan, St Thomas & St. Marten

1996   Retired from education, 38 years plus Air Force time. Grand Sentinel OES of Ohio

1998   Associate Grand Patron, OES & 1999 - Worthy Grand Patron, OES of Ohio

2001   Elected in October as a Grand Trustee for five years, Ohio Order of the Eastern Star

2002   Went to Portland, OR, 8 days for General Grand Chapter, Order of the Eastern Star

2003   Vacationing, golfing and taking it easy

2006   Moved to South Carolina, a new house in a Del Web community, Golf Course & etc.

2008   Finished writing my life story

*1946, Loren, Homer, Kenneth, George, Cartmal & Dad*

*Our Apartment, Htgtn, WV 1956*

Homer in front of Wagon, 1936

Sister Joyce and Homer, 1937

*Our House in KY, 1937*

*Out House in WV, 1942*

*Kenneth on Horse and Homer, 1947*

*Homer, Lincoln Co. HS band, 1946*

*Target Practice, Alaska, 1953*

GoingFishing. YukonR. 1954

*Fishing the Yukon, 1954*

*My first Car A 1951 Ford, Bought, 1955*

*Mother and Me, 1958*

*John, Tim, Gloria & Homer 1961, MA Degree*

*Cades Cove, Smoky Mts., 1967*

*Brothers & Sisters: Lorena, Ida Mae, Joyce, Mildred,*
*Loren, Kennth, Cartmal, George, Homer, 1972*

*Oak Hill Centennial, 1973*

*Gloria, Tim, Chris, Homer & Jon*

*Ohio Grand Line, OES, Homer, Gloria, Peggy Wright & Dave*
*Rio Grande U*

Ma _____ Tax for the year 1855.

For County purposes, _____ Tithes, Personal Property,
    White Male and Personal Property,         $ 1.31
    Revenue,            Tracts Land,        Acres,
For county purposes, 40 per cent. on same.

Received payment, _____

Ma _____ Tax in Scott County for 1860.

    White titheables, county levy, _____
    Black    do    do    do., _____
    Revenue—Slaves, personal property, $ _____ Capitation tax, }
        Salary, interest, &c., _____
        Land, _____
    Road levy, _____

Received the above in full, _____

*Property Tax Records, Great Grandfather Lawson, 1955, 1860,*
*VA*